LEGENDS OF THE GAME

100 FAMOUS SPORTS STARS

SAVITA PANDIT

TRUE SIGN
PUBLISHING HOUSE

Published by True Sign Publishing House
Address: 21, 2nd Floor, Kundan Nagar, Bagmugaliya,
Bhopal, Madhya Pradesh - 462026
E-mail: truesignbooks@gmail.com
Website: www.truesign.in

Legends Of The Game
100 Famous Sports Stars

Author: Savita Pandit

ISBN: 978-93-5988-086-0

First Edition: 2024

CONTENTS

1

MUHAMMAD ALI (BOXING)

Former American professional boxer and civil rights leader Muhammad Ali was born on January 17, 1942, in Louisville, Kentucky, United States. He passed away on June 3, 2016, in Scottsdale, Arizona. After being the first boxer to do it three times, Ali went on to successfully defend his world heavyweight championship a total of nineteen times.

Public spaces in the United States were segregated while Cassius Marcellus Clay, Jr. was a child growing up in the South. His dad, Cassius Marcellus Clay, Sr., painted signs and billboards to help support his family. His mom, Odessa Grady Clay, was a housekeeper.

Louisville police officer Joe Martin mentored 12-year-old Clay in the sport of boxing. He started his professional career under the tutelage of the Louisville Sponsoring Group, a syndicate of eleven rich white men, after rising through the amateur ranks and winning the 175-pound class gold medal in the 1960 Olympic Games in Rome.

When Clay started fighting professionally, his charisma and charismatic demeanour were more respected than his boxing prowess. To get people interested in his battles, he would recite naive poetry and use self-deprecating expressions like "float like a butterfly, sting like a bee." The harsh reality of boxing seemed to contradict his claims of being "the Greatest," which he proudly shared with the world. For all the admiration he received, Clay enraged sports fans. He seemed to be devoid of genuine knockout power, had an unusually low hand position, and retreated from blows instead of ducking and weaving to avoid harm. He was defeating fighters who had never been better than ordinary, as well as veterans who were well beyond their prime. Because of this, purists felt sick to their stomachs whenever Clay made predictions about which round, he would knock out an opponent, and they grimaced even more when he really accomplished it and boasted about his victories.

Over time, Ali's religious ideas also changed. He embraced Orthodox Islam and started studying the Quran diligently in the mid-1970s. A spiritual embracing of all people and preparation for his own afterlife replaced his prior allegiance to the teachings of Elijah Muhammad, such as the idea that white people are "devils" and that there is neither heaven nor hell. "What he teaches is not at all what we believe in," Ali openly said in 1984 in opposition to Louis Farrakhan's separatist ideology. We would rather not be identified with him since he symbolizes the period when we were struggling in the dark and confused as individuals.

Lonnie, whose maiden name was Yolanda Williams, became Ali's fourth wife in 1986. The majority of Ali's nine children shied away from the limelight that he so enjoyed. But his daughter Laila Ali had a successful professional boxing career, winning several weight class championships and going unbeaten in 24 fights from 1999 to 2007.

In 1996, at the XXVI Olympiad in Atlanta, Georgia, Ali was selected to ignite the Olympic torch before the games began. His arrival was greeted with an outpouring of kindness that solidified his position as one of the world's most adored sportsmen. The film Ali (2001) was based on his turbulent life from 1964 to 1974 and stars Will Smith as the boxer. I Am Ali (2014) is a documentary that tells his life narrative via interviews with close associates and audio recordings he made over his career. Both the 2019 docuseries What's My Name and the 2021 film Muhammad Ali, which Burns co-directed, focused on him. Among Ali's many accolades are the 2005 Presidential Medal of Freedom and his 1990 induction into the International Boxing Hall of Fame.

2

MICHAEL JORDAN (BASKETBALL)

Michael Jordan is a legendary American basketball player who played at the college and professional levels. He was born on February 17, 1963, in Brooklyn, New York, USA. During his tenure as head coach, the Chicago Bulls won six NBA titles (1991–1993, 1996–1998).

After attending UNC Chapel Hill in 1981, Jordan moved to Wilmington, North Carolina, where he spent his childhood. In the 1982 national championship game, he scored the game-winning shot against Georgetown while only a freshman. Jordan left North Carolina following his junior year after being awarded the conference's best player both years. Under his direction, the United States basketball team won gold in the 1984 and 1992 Summer Olympics in Los Angeles and Barcelona, Spain, respectively.

The Chicago Bulls selected Jordan in the 1984 NBA Draft. He was voted Rookie of the Year and led the league in scoring in his first professional season (1984–85). He missed most of the next season due to a fractured foot, but he came back to lead the NBA in scoring for seven straight seasons, averaging about 33 points per game. In the 1986–87 season, he joined Wilt Chamberlain as the only player to earn 3,000 points. Five times (1988, 1991, 1992, 1996, and 1998), Jordan was voted the NBA's MVP. In 1988, he was also named the league's defensive player of the year. After guiding the Bulls to their third straight title in October 1993, Jordan took a short break from basketball to play professional baseball. March 1995 saw his comeback to the basketball court. Jordan guided the Bulls to an NBA-record 72-10 regular season record in 1995–96; the Warriors broke the mark in 2015–16. Once again, the Bulls won three straight titles under Jordan's leadership from 1996 to 1998, and he was awarded NBA Finals MVP each year. Another retirement for Jordan after the 1997–98 season.

By purchasing a part in the Washington Wizards in January of 2000, Jordan maintained a connection to the sport. As for the club's basketball operations, he was also named President. Jordan, nevertheless, felt that playing on the court was more important than overseeing the Wizards' rosters and wage limits. Thus, he relinquished his ownership and managerial roles in September 2001. After seeing a decline in attendance and broadcast ratings since his retirement in 1998, the NBA was eager to welcome him back for a second stint. The 2002–03 season was Jordan's last before he announced his retirement. He finished his career with 32,292 points, the second-highest total ever, and the greatest point-per-game average in league history at 30.12. He also had 2,514 steals. The Charlotte Bobcats, currently called the Charlotte Hornets, were an NBA team that Jordan joined in 2006 as a minority owner and general manager. In 2010, he became the first former NBA player to possess a majority stake in an NBA club when he purchased a controlling interest in the team.

Jordan was a very gifted shooter, passer, and fierce defender during his playing career. He stood at 6 feet 6 inches (1.98 meters) tall and played the position of guard. His incredible jumping ability and acrobatic maneuvers gained him the moniker "Air Jordan," and his fame reached levels never seen by sports or entertainers. Endorsements, especially for his iconic Air Jordan basketball sneakers, helped him amass millions of dollars. In 1996, he directed the hit picture Space Jam, which included Bugs Bunny and Daffy Duck, among other cartoon characters. The National Basketball Association selected him as one of the 50 all-time greats in 1996, and he was inducted into the Naismith Memorial Basketball Hall of Fame in 2009. In 2016, the President bestowed the Medal of Freedom upon him.

3

PELÉ (SOCCER)

Pelé was a Brazilian football (soccer) player who was perhaps the most renowned and highest-paid athlete of his time. He was born on October 23, 1940, in Três Corações, Brazil, and died on December 29, 2022, in São Paolo, Brazil. His three World Cup victories (1958, 1962, and 1970) were all with the Brazilian national team.

Major club clubs in São Paulo rejected Pelé after he played for a small league club in Bauru, São Paulo state (his nickname seems to have no meaning). But he became a part of the Santos Football Club in 1956. The team won nine São Paulo league titles and the Libertadores Cup and Intercontinental Club Cup in 1962 and 1963, respectively, with Pelé playing inside left striker. In Brazil, he gained legendary status as a national hero, earning him the nickname "Pérola Negra" ("Black Pearl"). He had an extraordinary knack for reading the actions of his teammates and kicking with both force and precision. In an effort to keep Pelé in Brazil after the 1958

World Cup, the Brazilian government designated him a national treasure, which effectively turned down huge offers from teams in Europe. During his 909th first-class encounter on November 19, 1969, he scored his 1,000th goal.

In 1957, Pelé made his debut for his country at the tender age of sixteen, and the following year, he participated in his first World Cup match in Sweden. The young Brazilian manager was apprehensive to start him at first. Pelé wasted little time making an impression upon entering the pitch, as he promptly set up a goal and rattled the post with a single shot. He scored twice in Brazil's 5-2 championship win against Sweden and a hat trick in the semifinal match against France. In the second match of the 1962 World Cup finals, Pelé tore a muscle in his thigh, forcing him to miss the rest of the tournament. Still, Brazil won the World Cup for the second time in its history. Pelé considered calling it quits in 1966 when his Brazil national team was eliminated in the first round due to rough play and injuries. In 1970, he made a triumphant return to the World Cup, this time with rising talents Rivelino and Jairzinho, helping Brazil win their third championship and cement their place as permanent holders of the Jules Rimet Trophy. With 12 goals in 14 games throughout his World Cup tenure, Pelé left no stone unturned.

Pelé became a global superstar because of his electric play and knack for incredible goals. To capitalize on his fame, his team, Santos, went on a world tour. When he and his squad went to Nigeria in 1967, the country's civil war was temporarily halted so that everyone could see the great player play.

After announcing his retirement in 1974, Pelé took a deal to promote soccer in the US and signed a three-year, $7 million deal with the North American Soccer League's New York Cosmos in 1975. After guiding the Cosmos to the 1977 league title, he decided to retire.

The 1978 International Peace Award went to Pelé. The French sports magazine L'Equipe named him Athlete of the Century in 1980, and the International Olympic Committee repeated the title in 1999. The Santos, Brazil, Pelé Museum was opened to the public in 2014. Aside from his sporting achievements, he was also the hero of several critically acclaimed documentaries and semi-documentaries and the author of multiple best-selling memoirs. The score for the 1977 film Pelé was one of several musical compositions he wrote.

4

SERENA WILLIAMS (TENNIS)

Serena Williams (born September 26, 1981, in Saginaw, Michigan, U.S.) inspired women's tennis with her strong style and won 23 Grand Slam singles championships during the open era.

Williams was raised in Compton. Her parents, nurse Oracine Price and security expert Richard Williams, and elder sister Venus Williams were in the family. Price has three daughters from prior marriages. Both parents pushed Serena and Venus Williams to play tennis, but Richard Williams coached them on local public courts. The sisters practiced for hours under his harsh coaching. To enroll Serena and Venus Williams at a tennis school, the family travelled to Florida in 1991. Serena Williams became a pro in 1995, one year after her sister. They gained prominence for their booming serves, ground strokes, and quickness. Serena Williams won the 1999 U.S. Open, defying predictions that Venus would do so. The sisters won the doubles event at that tournament and won 14 Grand Slam doubles championships together.

In Sydney, Australia, Serena and Venus Williams won doubles gold in the 2000 Olympics. After years of inconsistency, Serena Williams won the French Open, Wimbledon, and U.S. Open in 2002, beating Venus Williams in the finals. At the latter event, Serena Williams' catsuit drew notice. Williams, a fashion enthusiast, was known for her daring ensembles that showed her power and defied conventional dress norms. In 2003, Williams won the Australian Open, completing a career Grand Slam by winning all four slam titles. In 2003, she won Wimbledon and both Grand Slams after defeating her sister in the finals. Williams won the Australian Open again in 2005. After a year of recovery, she won her third Australian Open in 2007. In Beijing, Serena and Venus Williams won their second Olympic doubles gold medal. Later that year, Williams won her third U.S. Open. She won her 10th Grand Slam singles championship in the 2009 Australian Open. Later that year, she defeated her sister again to win her third Wimbledon singles championship. Williams defended her Australian Open and Wimbledon crowns in 2010. Several health difficulties kept her off the court for over a year.

Williams won her fifth Wimbledon singles championship in 2012. She became the second woman (after Steffi Graf) to clinch a lifetime Golden Slam with a singles gold medal at the London Olympics a month later. She won doubles alongside her sister. Later that year, Williams won her 15th Grand Slam singles championship at the U.S. Open. She won her second French Open and sixth U.S. Open in 2013. After defending her U.S. Open title in 2014, Williams tied Chris Evert and Martina Navratilova for the second-most Grand Slam championships in the open era with 18. The following year, she won her sixth Australian Open. Williams won her 20th Grand Slam singles title at the 2015 French Open. She won her sixth Wimbledon singles gold in a straight-set final to extend her hot trend. Williams won Wimbledon again in 2016, tying Graf for the Grandest Slam singles championships in the open era for women and men. Williams beat her sister in the 2017 Australian Open final to break Graf's record.

5

USAIN BOLT (TRACK AND FIELD)

Jamaican sprinter Usain Bolt is generally regarded as the best of all time; he broke the Olympic record by winning gold in the 100-meter and 200-meter events at the same Olympics in three consecutive years. Bolt was born on August 21, 1986, in Montego Bay, Jamaica.

As a preteen cricket fast bowler, Bolt—the son of grocers in the remote Trelawny parish of Jamaica—gave his all. Despite his growing devotion to Real Madrid and Manchester United, two European football (soccer) clubs, he was encouraged by his school instructors to pursue track and field. It was during the 2002 World Junior Championships that Bolt first established himself as a track prodigy. At the age of fifteen, Bolt became the youngest male world junior champion in history when he won the 200-meter race at that meet, which took place in Kingston, Jamaica, in front of an audience of 36,000. Having lowered the junior (those aged 19 and under) 200-meter world record to 20.13 seconds when he was 16 years old, Bolt became the first teenager to run the event in sub-20 seconds when he ran the same event in 19.93 seconds when he was 17 years old. But a hamstring injury prevented him from competing in the 2004 Olympics in Athens beyond the 200-meter heats, and he finished dead last in the 2005 final of the global track and field championships.

Despite the common belief that sprinters with a height of 6 feet 5 inches (1.96 meters) have an edge when it comes to starting quickly, Bolt proved that theory wrong. He won silver in the 200-meter event in the 2007 world championships, when he seemed to have suddenly become more committed to his preparation. In his first professional 100-meter race, he managed to convince his coach to give him a go, and he finished in 10.03 seconds. He set a new world record of 9.76 seconds on May 3, 2008, which was the second-fastest performance at the time. Bolt defeated world champion Tyson Gay in a 9.72-second dash four weeks later in New York City, shattering the world mark.

Bolt achieved a first in the 2008 Olympic Games by becoming the first man since American Carl Lewis in 1984 to win the 100 meters, 200 meters, and 4 × 100-meter relay in the same Olympics. He also established a world mark in all three events, with times of 9.69 seconds, 19.30 seconds, and 37.10 seconds, respectively. The removal of Bolt's gold medal from the 4 × 100 event was caused by a teammate who failed a drug test. His victory margin in the 200-meter race was 0.66 seconds, which was the biggest in Olympic history. In the 100-meter race, he had a 0.20-second lead over the runner-up, even though he started celebrating approximately 80 meters into the race. This was the biggest gap since Lewis won by the same amount. Bolt won the 100-meter final at the 2009 World Championships in 9.58 seconds, shattering his own record. At the global championships four days later, he won a second gold medal after shattering his personal best in the 200-meter race by the same margin of 0.11 seconds.

At the 2011 World Championships, Bolt was considered a big favorite in the sprint events; however, he was disqualified from the 100-meter final due to a false start. Bolt nevertheless managed to win the 200-meter and 4 × 100-meter relays, even if he didn't take home a medal in his famous race. In the latter, he even helped create a new world record. Defending his 100-meter and 200-meter championships in the 2012 London Olympics, Bolt became the first athlete to accomplish so in successive Olympiads. He established a new Olympic record in the 100-meter event. At the 2013 global championships, he took home three gold medals in the 100-meter, 200-meter, and 4 × 100-meter relay events.

6

DIEGO MARADONA (SOCCER)

Born on October 30, 1960, in Lanus, Buenos Aires, Argentina, Diego Maradona was an Argentine football (soccer) player who is widely considered the best of all time and the best of the 1980s.

He passed away on November 25, 2020, in Tigre, Buenos Aires. Famous for his superb ball control and knack for setting up teammates for goals, he captained Argentina, Italy, and Spain to club titles and was a key member of the 1986 World Cup-winning Argentina national squad.

Early on, Maradona showed promise as a football player, and he joined the boys' squad Las Cebollitas ("The Little Onions") when he was eight years old. The team won 136 games in a row and the national title. He joined Argentinos Juniors when he was fourteen years old and debuted in the top division ten days before he turned sixteen in 1976. Just four months after that, he became the youngest Argentine to ever make his national team debut. Despite his exclusion from the 1978 World Cup-winning squad due to his youth, he guided the national under-20 team to a Junior World Cup title the following year.

After joining Boca Juniors in 1981, Maradona had an instant impact, leading the team to victory. After a successful stint in Spain with FC Barcelona (1982–1983), he went to Italy to play with SSC Napoli (1984–1991), where he helped propel a historically underachieving Naples club to the pinnacle of Italian football. The squad won the league championship in 1990 and the cup in 1987 when Maradona was on the club. After Maradona's 15-month sentence for cocaine possession led to his arrest in Argentina, his time with Napoli came to an end. He then moved on to play for Argentine club Newell's Old Boys and Spanish club Sevilla. From 1995 until his last match on October 25, 1997, he was a member of Boca Juniors.

The Argentine national team, during Maradona's tenure there, participated in the World Cup four times: in 1982, 1986, 1990, and 1994. At the 1986 Mexico competition, he was unstoppable. When his team beat England 2-1 in the quarterfinals, he scored two of the most iconic goals in World Cup history. His hand was used to score the first, which is now known as the "Hand of God" goal since the referee believed the ball had hit his head instead. The second goal came when Maradona took the ball in the middle of the pitch, dribbled past a swarm of English defenders and then slotted it past the custodian. After testing positive for the substance ephedrine, he was banned for the second time and did not complete the 1994 World Cup. In 1987 and 1989, Maradona was a member of the South American championship-winning squads.

Maradona, a lanky but dogged midfielder, became a hero to the working class in Argentina (his birthplace) and southern Italy (where he captained Napoli to triumph over the more affluent northern teams). Throughout his 21-year professional career, he appeared in 490 official club games, scoring 259 goals. He made 91 appearances for Argentina, scoring 34 goals in that time. The Fédération Internationale de Football Association held an online vote in which Maradona was ranked as the best player of the twentieth century.

As of 2008, Maradona was leading the Argentine national squad as its head coach. He led Argentina to the quarterfinals of the 2010 World Cup, but his time as head coach came to an end after he and the country's football governing body were unable to reach a contract extension. As of 2011, Maradona was the head coach of Al Wasl of the UAE. Unfortunately, Maradona was let go the next year due to the team's struggles. Prior to joining the Dorados de Sinaloa coaching staff in Mexico in 2018, he had experience with a number of different teams.

7

CRISTIANO RONALDO (SOCCER)

Cristiano Ronaldo, one of the best soccer players of all time, was born on February 5, 1985, in Funchal, Madeira, Portugal. He is of Portuguese descent.

Ronaldo's dad, José Dinis Aveiro, worked as the Andorinha club's equipment manager. (When Cristiano was born, his father wanted him to be named after Ronald Reagan, the American president at the time, as Reagan was Cristiano's favorite actor.) Ronaldo had heart surgery when he was 15 years old, but he was only out for a short time and eventually returned to full health. Before making his professional debut with Sporting Clube de Portugal (now known as Sporting Lisbon), he played for Clube Desportivo Nacional of Madeira. After making the switch, he spent time with Sporting Lisbon's junior squads.

At 6 feet 1 inch (1.85 meters) tall, Ronaldo was an imposing athlete on the field. He evolved from a right winger into a striker with a reckless style of play. With a deft touch, he could fool his opponents into giving him enough room to find cracks in their defenses.

Ronaldo joined English superpower Manchester United in 2003 after a great season with Sporting, which drew him to the attention of Europe's best football teams. His meteoric rise to stardom coincided with widespread recognition of him as a top-tier striker. The 2007–08 season was his best at United; he scored 42 goals in all competitions (League, Cup, and Golden Shoe) and was named Europe's top scorer (31 goals in the league). In May 2008, Ronaldo helped United win the Champions League. He had an outstanding 2007–08 season and was named FIFA World Player of the Year. United also made it to the 2009 Champions League final under his leadership, although they were defeated by FC Barcelona.

Real Madrid of Spain, a club Ronaldo had long been linked to, paid a record-breaking £80 million (about $131 million) to get him shortly after. Even after joining a new club, he remained to be a prolific scorer, setting a La Liga record for most goals scored in a season with 40 in 2010–11. Only the next season did his rival Lionel Messi of Barcelona surpass him. Ronaldo had a career year in 2011–12 when he scored 46 goals for Real Madrid and helped them win La Liga. He won his second global player of the year title in 2013 after scoring 66 goals in 56 games for Madrid and the Portuguese national team. The FIFA Global Player of the Year was changed to the FIFA Ballon d'Or in 2010. After leading Real Madrid to the Champions League triumph in 2014 with 52 goals in 43 games, Ronaldo won the Ballon d'Or once again. He was the league's leading scorer in 2014–15 with 48 goals. Ronaldo became Real Madrid's all-time top scorer in October 2015 after he scored his 324th goal for the club. In 2015–16, he helped Real win the Champions League for the record eleventh time and scored 35 goals in La Liga. He received his fourth Ballon d'Or in December 2016 for all of his achievements. In 2016–17, Ronaldo won a record-tying 42 goals for Real Madrid in all competitions, helping his side win La Liga and the Champions League. He also won his fifth Ballon d'Or trophy. With his 44 goals in 44 games in 2017–18, Real Madrid won their third consecutive Champions League.

8

MICHAEL PHELPS (SWIMMING)

American swimmer Michael Phelps set a record with 28 medals, including 23 gold, and was the most decorated athlete in Olympic history. He was born on June 30, 1985, in Baltimore, Maryland, United States. He broke the record for most Olympic gold medals won by an athlete in a single Games when he won eight in Beijing in 2008.

Phelps joined the elite North Baltimore Aquatic Club when he was seven years old; he came from a long line of swimmers. In the 200-meter butterfly event at the Sydney 2000 Olympics, he came in fifth place. At the 2001 U.S. spring nationals, he set a new world record in the 200-meter butterfly at the age of 15, becoming the youngest male swimmer to do so. His time was 1 minute, 54.92 seconds. At the next year's global championships in Fukuoka, Japan, he won his first international title. Among his five medals at the 2002 Pan Pacific championships, he took home three golds in the 200-meter and 400-meter individual medley events, as well as in the 4 × 100-meter medley relay. Breaking five individual world records in the 2003 world championships in Barcelona, Spain, he made history at the 2003 U.S. spring nationals by becoming the first male swimmer to win titles in three separate strokes at a single national championship. Phelps also set a record in the U.S. summer championships by winning five titles—more than any male swimmer in the history of the event.

In the 2004 Summer Olympics in Athens, Phelps won six gold medals (in the 200-meter and 400-meter individual medley, 100-meter and 200-meter butterfly, 4 × 200-meter freestyle, and 4 × 100-meter medley relay events), two bronze medals (in the 200-meter freestyle and 4 × 100-meter freestyle relay events), and set five records, both at the Olympic and world levels. When he won four gold medals in individual swimming at the 1972 Munich Olympics, he equaled the record established by American Mark Spitz. Phelps maintained his dominance of the sport in the 2007 world championships in Melbourne when he established five world records and won seven gold medals in several events (200-meter and 400-meter individual medley, 100-meter and 200-meter butterfly, 200-meter freestyle, and 4 × 100-meter and 4 × 200-meter freestyle relays). When it came to large international meets, Phelps equaled Spitz for most victories with seven.

Phelps' first event at the 2012 London Olympics, the 400-meter individual medley, was a letdown, as he did not earn a medal. On the other hand, he went on to win silver in the 200-meter butterfly and the 4 × 100-meter freestyle relay, as well as a gold in the 4 × 200-meter freestyle relay. By taking home the latter gold, Phelps broke the record held by Soviet gymnast Larisa Latynina and became the first athlete in Olympic history to accomplish the feat. In addition to his three straight 100-meter butterfly victories, he made history by winning gold in the 200-meter individual medley at the Olympics, making him the first male swimmer to do so. The 4 × 100-medley relay was Phelps' last event before retiring from swimming, and he won a gold medal in it. He had declared his retirement after the London Games.

9

ROGER FEDERER (TENNIS)

Tennis great Roger Federer, who was born on August 8, 1981, in Basel, Switzerland, ruled the court at the turn of the millennium thanks to his superb all-around performance. He became the first player to win 20 Grand Slam men's singles championships in 2018, and he set a record by winning eight Wimbledon crowns.

Beginning his tennis career at the tender age of eight, Federer went on to win the Swiss junior title at the tender age of fourteen. He won the Orange Bowl junior event in Miami in 1998 and the Wimbledon junior singles title the same year. After making his Davis Cup debut the following year, Federer became the youngest tennis player to ever complete a season in the top 100, ending at number 64. He was 18 years and four months old.

Federer reached the bronze medal match during his Olympic competition in Sydney in 2000. He reached the semifinals of Wimbledon the following year after beating Pete Sampras, and he was ranked sixth in the world at the end of 2002. Federer won Wimbledon in 2003, his first Grand Slam competition. He won the Australian Open and the U.S. Open and successfully defended his Wimbledon championship the following year. In addition to his skill as a shot creator, his forehand earned him a reputation for coolness under pressure and good sportsmanship. With a perfect record of 11 wins out of 17 events played in 2004, Roger Federer concluded the year atop the global rankings. Similarly impressive were his 2005 statistics, as he won eleven of fifteen events (including Wimbledon and the U.S. Open). Additionally, he won a record-breaking 24 consecutive finals from July 2003 to November 2005.

As 2006 came to a close, Federer remained unrivalled. In addition to his Wimbledon victory, he also won the Australian Open and the U.S. Open, making history as the first player to accomplish it for three consecutive years. Additionally, he lost in the finals against Spain's Rafael Nadal at Roland Garros, the French Open. With the exception of one tournament, Federer participated in 17 events in 2006, winning 12 championships and making it to the finals in every one of them. He won his tenth Grand Slam championship in 2007 at the Australian Open. But in that year, Nadal once again thwarted his attempt to win the French Open, this time in the final. In 2007, at Wimbledon, Federer and Nadal maintained their battle. After a nail-biting five-set final against Nadal, he became only the second male player in almost a century to win Wimbledon five times in a row, after Björn Borg. In 2007, Federer extended his record of men's open-era dominance by winning the U.S. Open for the fourth year in a row.

Federer won the French Open for the first time in June 2009, completing his career with a Grand Slam title in every one of the four events. Win number fourteen for Federer, tying him for second all-time with Pete Sampras. In a nail-biting five-set encounter that lasted 5-7, 7-6, 7-6, 3-6, 16-14, Federer won his sixth Wimbledon championship and a record 15th Grand Slam trophy for his career the following month at Wimbledon. He went on to recover the world's number-one status. He beat British player Andy Murray to win the Australian Open in January 2010. In 2012, Federer won his seventh Wimbledon championship, matching his career record, after defeating Murray once again. The men's gold medal match in the London Olympics took place one month later. Nevertheless, Federer was defeated by Murray and was only awarded the silver medal this time.

10

TIGER WOODS (GOLF)

Born on December 30, 1975, in Cypress, California, USA, American golfer Tiger Woods became the first player in the sport's history to win the same four major events in a row in the late '90s and early '00s. One of golf's all-time greats, Woods made history in 1997 when he became the first player of African American or Asian origin to win the Masters Tournament. With four more wins, he would tie Jack Nicklaus for second place all-time at the Masters.

In 2019, U.S. President Donald Trump presented Woods with the Presidential Medal of Freedom, adding to his many accolades. Afterwards, the T.V. documentary Tiger (2021) focused on him.

The father of Woods's family is African American, while his mother is Thai. He began playing golf at an early age and quickly became a prodigy, taking swings for a T.V. show at the tender age of two and scoring a nine-hole score of 48 at the tender age of three. He had one of the best amateur golf careers ever after becoming the youngest champion of the U.S. Junior Amateur Championship in 1991 at the tender age of fifteen. One of his three straight U.S. Amateur Championships was in 1994 when he recovered from a six-hole deficit to claim victory. He became a Stanford University student in 1994 and a collegiate champion the following year. On August 29, 1996, Woods went professional after winning his third U.S. Amateur championship. He then quit college. He was voted Rookie of the Year by the PGA Tour in 1996 after competing professionally in eight PGA tournaments and winning two championships.

Woods often struck shots over 300 yards due to his ability to create club speed. Fans and opponents alike were intimidated by his towering long game, excellent putting and chipping, and reputation for mental fortitude. Woods had one of the most dominant performances in professional golf history in the 1997 Masters Tournament in Augusta, Georgia. He scored a tournament record 270 over 72 holes and finished 12 shots clear of the field. For the first time in over 20 years, he won eight PGA events in a single year in 1999. Between 1999 and 2000, he won six in a row, tying Ben Hogan for the second-longest run in PGA history; the record is held by Byron Nelson with eleven straight wins. Woods won the U.S. Open for the second time in June of 2000, shattering his own record in the process. The greatest winning margin in a major event was 15 strokes, and Woods became the first player to complete the tournament at 12 under par. He tied Nicklaus for the lowest 72-hole total with 272.

Woods won the British Open on July 23, 2000, making him the fifth and youngest player in golf history to do it. He had already won all four majors in his career. (The four main events in 1930 were the U.S. Open, the British Open, the U.S. Amateur, and the British Amateur championships. Bobby Jones won the lone Grand Slam that year.) With a record-setting 19 shots under par, Woods cruised to an 8-stroke triumph. He won the Masters Tournament in 2001 and again in 2002. Woods made history in 2001 when he won the Masters Tournament, becoming the first player to do it in a row. He had previously won the U.S. Open, the British Open (Open Championship), the PGA Championship, and the Masters. We called it the "Tiger Slam."

11

BABE RUTH (BASEBALL)

New York, New York, was the site of Babe Ruth's death on August 16, 1948. Ruth was born on February 6, 1895, in Baltimore, Maryland, United States. Between 1919 and 1935, Ruth hit a record number of home runs, which helped propel him to the status of possibly the most revered athlete in American history.

His humble beginnings contributed to the aura that surrounded Ruth. Ruth had a tough upbringing, even if the story about him being an orphan is not genuine. His German-speaking, working-class parents were George Herman Ruth, Sr. and Kate Shamberger Ruth. In a rough area near the river in Baltimore, Ruth Sr. ran a tavern. The Ruths lived in quarters above the bar and had eight children; however, only the eldest, George Jr. and a younger sister made it to maturity. George had many brushes with the police, smoked tobacco, skipped school multiple times, and participated in petty theft, as neither his father nor his ailing mother had much time for the child. His parents entrusted him to the care of the Xaverian Brothers, a Roman Catholic order, at St. Mary's Industrial School for Boys in Baltimore, Maryland, in 1902. Ruth spent the next decade coming and going from St. Mary's. A lifelong ward of the school, he became so after his mother's death from TB in 1912.

Ruth may have escaped poverty and oblivion if she had played baseball. Jack Dunn, owner of the local minor-league Baltimore Orioles organization, signed him to a $600 contract in 1914 after he became famous in his hometown for his baseball skills as a youngster at St. Mary's. When a sportswriter called Ruth one of "Dunn's babes," Ruth became known as "Babe." Ruth was a big guy for his day; he weighed over 200 pounds and was over six feet tall. Dunn traded Ruth to the Boston Red Sox of the American League before the 1914 season ended because of his outstanding pitching performance. Helen Woodford, a waitress, was Ruth's sweetheart the same year they met.

As time went on, Ruth established herself as baseball's top left-handed pitcher. I won three World Series games (one in 1916 and two in 1918) and set a record by throwing 292/3 straight shutout innings during a stretch of scoreless World Series innings. He won 87 games between 1915 and 1919 and had an astounding earned run average of under 2.16.

Meanwhile, manager Ed Barrow used Ruth at first base or outfield on days when he did not pitch because of his impressive hitting power. At a time when they were uncommon, Ruth hit 29 home runs in 1919, breaking the record established by Ned Williamson of the Chicago White Stockings in 1884 for a single season. The perpetually strapped club owner and Broadway play producer Harry Frazee sold Ruth to the New York Yankees in 1920 for $125,000 plus a personal loan from Jacob Ruppert, another Yankee owner. Ruth was hesitant to leave Boston at first, but he eventually agreed to a two-year, $10,000-per-year deal with the Yankees.

12

JACKIE ROBINSON (BASEBALL)

Jackie Robinson was the first Black baseball player to play in the American big leagues during the 20th century. She was born on January 31, 1919, in Cairo, Georgia, U.S., and died on October 24, 1972, in Stamford, Connecticut. As a member of the National League Brooklyn Dodgers, Robinson tore down the decades-old "color line" in Major League Baseball on April 15, 1947. From 1947 to 1956, he was a Dodger, seeing action in both the infield and the outfield.

Robinson, who grew up in Pasadena, California, excelled in a variety of sports while attending Pasadena Junior College and UCLA. In addition to baseball, he was a standout on the football, basketball, and track teams. While still a third-year student at UCLA, Robinson dropped out in 1941 to assist his mother with household chores. He started playing semi-professional football in Hawaii and worked construction to help support his family. He enlisted in the United States Army in 1942 and went through officer candidate training; in

1943, he was promoted to the rank of second lieutenant. When ordered to sit in the rear of a military bus, Robinson defied orders and faced a court-martial in 1944. Robinson was granted an honorable discharge when the allegations against him were dropped. However, the event foreshadowed Robinson's eventual involvement in civil rights action. Branch Rickey, president and general manager of the Brooklyn Dodgers, took notice of him while he was playing professional baseball with the Negro American League's Kansas City Monarchs after he left the army.

In search of the ideal candidate, Rickey had been plotting an effort to integrate baseball. Rickey was really drawn to Robinson because of his athletic prowess, honesty, and traditional family values. Rickey was most concerned that Robinson would react negatively to the racial insults and undermine the effectiveness of integration efforts. Rickey wanted to make sure that Robinson could take insults well, so he yelled abuses at Robinson at a famous meeting. Robinson joined the Montreal Royals of the International League, a Dodgers farm club, on October 23, 1945, after being signed by Rickey.

After leading the league in hitting average in 1946, Brooklyn promoted Robinson to the major leagues in 1947. On the field, he had an instant impact. He was named MLB's first Rookie of the Year after leading the NL in stolen bases. With a hitting average of.342, he was named the National League MVP in 1949 and won the batting title.

He had had quite diverse experiences in his own life. He was the target of insults and bottles thrown by fans. Opposing players intentionally threw balls at Robinson's head and spiked him with their shoes during violent slides into bases, while other Dodger teammates publicly objected to playing alongside an African American. Robinson did not have his detractors among baseball players. The St. Louis Cardinals' players were about to go on strike if Robinson was to play, but Commissioner Ford Frick put a halt to the walkout by saying that the club would punish any player who participated. When the booing from fans became too much, Dodger captain Pee Wee Reese stepped off the field to rally behind Robinson, and the two became fast friends. But Robinson's historic major league career was marred by death threats, racist comments, and Jim Crow regulations that prevented a Black player from eating at the same restaurants as his teammates or staying in the same motels. During this time, Robinson had what he called a "starry" baseball career. He swung a.311 during his career and was a key figure in the Dodgers' six league titles and World Series triumph. Because of his base-stealing antics, Robinson frightened infielders and unsettled opposing pitchers.

13

LIONEL MESSI (SOCCER)

Born in Rosario, Argentina, Lionel Messi, a Soccer player of Argentine descent, won an unprecedented eight Ballon d'Or trophies as the best male player in the world (2009–12, 2015, 2019, 2021, and 2023). His contributions were important in Argentina's 2022 FIFA World Cup victory.

Messi joined the youth squad of Newell's Old Boys, a top-division football club headquartered in Rosario, in 1995 after beginning to play the sport as a youngster. Many elite clubs across the Atlantic were captivated by Messi's extraordinary talents. After moving to Barcelona with his family when he was thirteen years old, Messi joined FC Barcelona's under-14 squad. With a goal-scoring average of 21 in 14 games for the youth squad, he swiftly advanced to the senior squad and made his informal debut in a friendly match for FC Barcelona when he was 16 years old.

Messi became the youngest official player and goal scorer in the 2004–05 Spanish La Liga season when he was 17 years old. He was powerful, balanced, and adaptable despite being short in stature (only 5 feet 7 inches, or 1.7 meters) and hefty (148 pounds, or 67 kg). Messi was a gifted passer who could easily get past crowded opponents thanks to his left foot, speed, and control of the ball. The much-loved Catalans who root for Barcelona had mixed emotions when he was awarded Spanish citizenship in 2005. Messi and Barcelona won the Champions League the next year, which is the European club championship.

After steadily rising to prominence over the years, Lionel Messi was widely considered to be among the world's best players in 2008, when he was nominated for the Ballon d'Or but ultimately came in second place behind Cristiano Ronaldo of Manchester United. Midway through the 2008–09 season, Messi helped FC Barcelona win La Liga, the Copa del Rey (Spain's main domestic cup), and the Champions League, capping off an incredible 2008–09 season. This was the first "treble" for the club. His 38 goals in 51 games that season set a new record, and he easily beat Ronaldo in the Ballon d'Or and FIFA global Player of the Year voting. Messi led Barcelona to a repeat La Liga title in 2009–10 with 34 goals in domestic games. In addition to winning the Golden Shoe for top scorer in Europe, he was also named Ballon d'Or (the honor was called the FIFA Ballon d'Or from 2010 to 2015).

Messi was a global superstar in his own right, even when he wasn't playing football. Along with his football pay, which was consistently among the top two in all of professional sports (tied with Ronaldo's), he was also a very effective commercial endorser, most notably for Adidas. Messi and his father, who was in control of his son's money, faced tax fraud charges in 2013. They were accused of hiding their endorsement payments from Spain, which amounted to €4.2 million, by using offshore shell companies. The two were nonetheless compelled to face trial on the accusations in 2016, even though they paid €5 million to the Spanish state thereafter. The same year, in July, Messi and his father were fined €1.5 million and handed 21 months of suspended jail terms (in Spain, first-time offenders get suspended sentences if the length is less than two years).

14

LEBRON JAMES (BASKETBALL)

National Basketball Association (NBA) championships were won by the Miami Heat (2012), the Cleveland Cavaliers (2016), and the Los Angeles Lakers (2020)—LeBron James, an American professional basketball player, was born on December 30, 1984, in Akron, Ohio, USA. He is generally regarded as one of the best versatile players of all time. He surpassed Kareem Abdul-Jabbar's record of 38,387 points in 2023 to become the NBA's all-time top scorer.

Throughout his four years as a member of the Akron St. Vincent-St. Mary High School basketball team, James—a basketball prodigy in the area since elementary school—led the squad to three Ohio state titles and was crowned Ohio's Mr. Basketball three times. In his junior year, he made headlines around the country when he appeared on the cover of Sports Illustrated, a publication that referred to him as "The Chosen One." After James was named the best high school player in the country by a unanimous vote during his senior year, the Cleveland Cavaliers took him in the first round of the 2003 NBA draft. Even before he played a professional game, he inked a record-breaking $90 million endorsement deal with Nike.

James won the league's Rookie of the Year title in 2003–04 while leading the Cavaliers in scoring, steals, and minutes played, all while dealing with the expectations of these unique circumstances. James, a 6-foot-8" (2.03-meter) "point forward" who was equally comfortable distributing the ball down the floor or playing close to the basket, was an unusual threat to his opponents' basketball teams. His physique and speed were so impressive that he could have played football at the professional level.

After his contract with the Cavaliers ended at the conclusion of the 2009–10 season, James became one of the most sought-after, if not the most sought-after, free agents in NBA history. He embarked on a protracted courting with many clubs, some of whom had planned for his free agency for more than two years. Many felt that James's historic hour-long TV special was too ostentatious when he announced his deal with the Heat. Even though the Heat lost the NBA title to the Mavericks, he was a key contributor in their run to the finals in his first season. During the 2011–12 NBA season, James led Miami to its second straight finals trip with an MVP performance that included an average of 27.1 points per game. Thanks to James's outstanding performance, which earned him the title of finals MVP, the Heat prevailed over the Oklahoma City Thunder to claim the trophy.

He had a career-best season in 2012–13, averaging 26.8 points, 7.3 assists, and 8.0 rebounds per game. His field-goal percentage was 565—quite an accomplishment considering how often he played away from the basket—but he still managed to make a respectable number of shots. In addition to receiving his fourth league MVP trophy that season, James was instrumental in Miami's 27-game winning streak—the second-longest in NBA history—during that season. Once again, James was crowned NBA Finals MVP after leading the Heat to a seven-game series victory against the San Antonio Spurs the following season. After leading the Heat to another NBA Finals trip the previous season, he maintained his outstanding performance the next year, raising his shooting percentage by 002. In the end, however, Miami couldn't overcome the Spurs in their five-game rematch.

15

SACHIN TENDULKAR (CRICKET)

Indian professional cricketer Sachin Tendulkar was born on April 24, 1973, in Bombay (now Mumbai), India. He is widely regarded as one of the best batters in cricket history. He made history in 2012 as the only cricketer ever to reach 100 hundreds (100 runs in an innings) while playing for his national team.

At the age of eleven, Tendulkar received his first bat. He set a new world record of 329 out of 664 in a school match when he was 14 years old using it. He became the youngest Test (international) Cricketer for India when he made his debut against Pakistan in Karachi in November 1989 at the age of 16 years 205 days; a year later, on his first-class debut for Bombay (Mumbai), he struck a century. Two centuries—148 in Sydney and 114 in Perth—and 179 against the West Indies in 1994 came from him when he was only 18 years old in Australia. At the tender age of 23, Tendulkar was appointed captain of his nation's squad in August 1996.

Despite India's elimination from the 1996 World Cup quarterfinals, Tendulkar finished with 523 runs, more than any other player in the competition. His exceptional play during the 1997–98 season earned him the top Indian athletic honor, the Rajiv Gandhi Khel Ratna Award, which he received in 1998. Not only did India lose to Australia in the 1999 World Cup, but they also lost badly in the series against South Africa and Australia later that year. They could not even make it beyond round six. On the other hand, Tendulkar was instrumental in his team's 2003 World Cup run to the finals. Tendulkar was chosen man of the tournament despite India's loss against Australia; he averaged 60.2.

The 35th century that Tendulkar achieved in Test cricket against Sri Lanka in December 2005 broke all previous records. Tendulkar was able to overtake Sunil Gavaskar, the prolific run scorer for India, in 125 Tests. As a batter, Tendulkar became the first to achieve 15,000 runs in Test play in November 2011, and he became the first player to record 15,000 runs in one-day international (ODI) play in June 2007. He became the first man to ever reach 200 runs in an innings in one-day international play a month later when he made a remarkable "double century" in a match against South Africa. The International Cricket Council (ICC) honored him with the title of Cricketer of the Year in 2010. Tendulkar achieved a record-breaking 100th international century in a one-day international match against Bangladesh in March 2012. This century included both Test (51 centuries) and one-day international (49 centuries) cricket. Later that year, he announced his retirement from one-day international cricket. In 2013, he finished his six-year stay with the Mumbai Indians in the Indian Premier League and then resigned from Test cricket. He finished his playing days with records for the most runs in a career (34,357) and the most runs in a Test (15,921). Tendulkar was one of the top batters in the game for much of his lengthy career. His sure-handiwork from the front and back foot and his laser-like focus on scoring runs earned him comparisons to Australia's Don Bradman.

As the first active athlete to enter the Rajya Sabha, the upper house of the Indian parliament, Tendulkar was nominated for the position in 2012 and served until 2018. He made history in 2014 when he became the first athlete to earn the Bharat Ratna, India's highest civilian accolade. The International Cricket Council Hall of Fame made Tendulkar a 2019 inductee.

16

WAYNE GRETZKY (ICE HOCKEY)

Many people believe Canadian ice hockey player Wayne Gretzky—born January 26, 1961, in Brantford, Ontario, Canada—to be the best player in NHL history.

At the age of 2.5, Gretzky started skating, and his father was the one who first taught him the game of hockey. On a beginner hockey team with boys aged 10 and 11, he was already named an all-star by the time he was six years old. He played his way up through the ranks of organized youth hockey until he set a Junior World Cup record for scoring in 1977 while being the youngest player in the tournament. Gretzky made the transition to professional hockey for the 1978–79 season, suiting up with the WHA's Indianapolis Racers. Quickly after joining the National Hockey League at the start of the 1979–80 season, his contract was purchased by the Edmonton Oilers. In four consecutive seasons—1983–84, 1984–85, 1986–87, and 1987–88—Gretzky captained the Oilers to the Stanley Cup as the team's center and captain. He was dealt to the Kings by the Edmonton Oilers after the 1987–88 season.

The once-physical sport was transformed by Gretzky's speed and deftness. His first year with the Oilers was a 137-point campaign, highlighted by 51 goals and 86 assists. He made history in the 1980–81 NHL season by averaging more than two points per game, a feat never before accomplished. He scored 212 points, established a new regular-season record for assists with 120, and led the NHL in scoring in 1981–82. (In 1985–86, he had 215 points and 163 assists, breaking both records.) From 1980–81 through 1986–87, and again in 1989–90, 1990–91, and 1993–94, Gretzky was the highest NHL scorer and received the Art Ross Memorial Trophy. He won the Hart Memorial Trophy, which is presented annually to the league's most valuable player, for the first time in 1989–90 and for eight years in a row (from 1979–80 to 1986–87).

Gretzky surpassed Gordie Howe in two categories: first, for career goals scored (801) and second, for total points scored (1850) in the National Hockey League. The former record was set early in the 1989–90 season. The St. Louis Blues acquired Gretzky from the Kings in a 1996 trade. He inked a deal with the New York Rangers after that season. In a 1997 game against the Anaheim Mighty Ducks, Gretzky recorded his 1,851st assist, breaking yet another record. He became the NHL player with the most assists.

Upon being elected into the Hockey Hall of Fame in 1999, Gretzky retired from professional hockey after the 1998–99 season. He has scored 894 goals and amassed 2,857 points throughout his career. Following his last game, the National Hockey League retired his jersey number, 99. In 2000, Gretzky became a minority owner of the Phoenix Coyotes of the National Hockey League. In 2005, he was also appointed head coach of the team. Gretzky was the head coach of the struggling Coyotes until 2009 when he also lost his financial share in the club due to bankruptcy and the NHL's takeover of the franchise. In 2016, he made a triumphant comeback to the Oilers franchise in the role of vice chairman and partner. But he became a TV expert after stepping down in 2021.

17

MARTINA NAVRATILOVA (TENNIS)

Martina Navratilova was a Czech American tennis player who was the undisputed champion of women's tennis in the '70s and '80s. She was born on October 18, 1956, in Prague, Czechoslovakia, which is now part of the Czech Republic.

Navratilova made her tennis tournament debut when she was only eight years old. Her 1975 Federation Cup-winning squad brought her worldwide renown; she was a left-handed player who ranked first in Czechoslovakia from 1972 to 1975. The Czech authorities had tried to restrict her tennis career, so she moved into exile in the U.S. that year. After having her Czech citizenship revoked, she applied for and received her American citizenship in 1981. She became a dual citizen in 2008 when she reclaimed her Czech citizenship.

Navratilova maintained a stable position among the top five female tennis players beginning in 1975. In 1978, she won the Virginia Slims and the women's singles final at Wimbledon, solidifying her maiden claim to the top spot. With her 1979 Wimbledon singles and doubles titles under her belt, she was once again the best player in the world.

In 1982, Navratilova had an impressive record of 90 victories out of 93 matches, which included 41 straight victories. She also won 15 tournaments, including the women's singles events at Wimbledon and the French Open. The next year, she swept the women's singles tournaments at the U.S. Open, Wimbledon, and the Australian Open, winning 86 of 87 matches. She started winning Grand Slam women's singles championships in 1983 at Wimbledon and went on to win six in a row. During the 1980s, her friendly rivalry with Chris Evert was at its peak as well. In 80 matches, Navratilova won 43 games by contrasting her serve-and-volley game with Evert's baseline technique. She became just the second player in modern tennis history to win 1,000 matches in 1986 in Filderstadt, West Germany.

By 1990, Navratilova had won a record nine Wimbledon women's singles titles (1978, 1979, 1982–87, 1990), two French Opens (1982, 1984), three Australian Opens (1981, 1983, 1985), four U.S. Opens (1983, 1984, 1986, 1987), and one Wimbledon. She became the first U.S. Open winner since 1970 to win a triple crown in 1987, adding the women's doubles and mixed doubles titles to her singles title. When Martina Navratilova won her 158th victory in 1992 in Chicago, she had amassed more titles than any other player in tennis history, regardless of gender. With 167 championships under her belt, she called it quits in singles competition after the 1994 season.

From 1997 to 1999, Navratilova was not a part of the tennis circuit, and she only played in a small number of doubles matches over the following two years. But in 2000, she made a triumphant comeback to the professional circuit, playing in the doubles event at Wimbledon and other events. She became a Tennis Hall of Famer that same year. To equal Billie Jean King for the most Wimbledon championships overall (20), she won the mixed doubles at Wimbledon in 2003, partnering Leander Paes. Navratilova became the oldest player to win Wimbledon with her triumph; she is 46 years old. She hung up her tennis racket in 2006 after taking first place in the mixed doubles event at the U.S. Open. She won 59 Grand Slam tournaments during her career, including 18 in singles, 31 in doubles, and 10 in mixed doubles.

Martina, Navratilova, and George Vecsey's book came out in 1985. In addition, she collaborated with Liz Nickles on a mystery series featuring the tennis champion-turned-sleuth Jordan Myles. Breaking Point (1996) and Killer Instinct followed The Total Zone (1994). As an out lesbian and an activist for homosexual rights, Navratilova was one of the first famous athletes to come out as a lesbian.

18

JESSE OWENS (TRACK AND FIELD)

Track and field athlete Jesse Owens was born on September 12, 1913, in Oakville, Alabama, United States. He died on March 31, 1980, in Phoenix, Arizona. Owens won four gold medals in the 1936 Berlin Olympics and established a world record in the running broad jump, commonly known as the long jump, which remained in effect for 25 years. Adolf Hitler's plan to showcase Aryan supremacy at the Olympics was thwarted by his four Olympic triumphs.

Owens won three events in the 1933 National Interscholastic Championships in Chicago when he was a high school student from Cleveland. Owens equaled the world record for the 100-yard dash (9.4 seconds) and broke it for the 200-yard dash (20.3 seconds), the 200-yard low hurdles (22.6 seconds), and the long jump (8.13 meters, or 26.67 feet) all on the same day, May 25, 1935, while competing for Ohio State University (Columbus) at a track-and-field meet at the University of Michigan (Ann Arbor) in the Western (later Big Ten) Conference.

Owens's stellar performances at the 1936 Berlin Olympics have gone down in history, thanks to his amazing 100-meter run (10.3

seconds, an Olympic record), 200-meter run (20.7 seconds, a world record), long jump (8.06 meters, or 26.4 feet), and 4 × 100-meter relay (39.8 seconds), as well as his off-track events. A well-known urban legend that developed around Owens' triumphs was the "snub," the idea that Hitler declined to shake hands with Owens because of his race. Actually, Hitler had already resolved not to publicly applaud any athlete by the time Owens won the 100-meter final on the second day of competition. The president of the International Olympic Committee was so upset that Hitler should publicly congratulate all of the winners—German and Finnish alike—before he left the stadium following the elimination of German competitors from the day's last event that he demanded that the chancellor of Germany do the same. The "snub" was reported in American periodicals by people who were unaware of the facts, and the myth developed over time.

The Berlin Olympics were politically fraught, but the German people admired Carl Ludwig ("Luz") Long, a long jumper from Germany, and he helped Owens overcome a poor start to the race. The news that his apparent practice leap was really his first try flummoxed Owens. He was so worried that he botched the second try. Long advised the American to place a towel in front of the take-off board before Owens' last leap. Owens soared from there, making it to the finals, where he won the gold medal by defeating Long, who would later become his close buddy.

When it came to all sprint distances recognized by the International Amateur Athletic Federation (IAAF; subsequently, the International Association of Athletics Federations), Owens held or shared the world record for a certain period. Following his time on the track, Owens was active in a variety of roles, including public relations, secretary of the Illinois State Athletic Commission, goodwill missions to India and East Asia for the United States Department of State, and boys' mentoring. Posthumously bestowed to Owens in 1990, the Congressional Gold Medal followed his 1976 Presidential Medal of Freedom.

19

CARL LEWIS (TRACK AND FIELD)

Born on July 1, 1961, in Birmingham, Alabama, United States, American track and field athlete Carl Lewis won nine gold medals in the 1980 and 1990 Olympics.

Although Lewis was eligible to participate in the United States in the 1980 Olympics, he sat out of the Moscow Games due to the country's boycott. In 1984, at the Los Angeles Games, Lewis was a part of the United States 4 × 100-meter relay team and won gold medals in the 100-meter (9.9 seconds) and 200-meter (19.8 seconds) events, as well as in the long jump (8.54 meters, or 28.02 feet). Among American track and field athletes, Lewis joined Alvin Kraenzlein (1900) and Jesse Owens (1936), who both won four gold medals in the same Olympics—in Berlin—that Lewis won in Los Angeles—making them the third and fourth such athletes, respectively.

Lewis became the first Olympic athlete to win consecutive long-jump gold medals with a leap of 8.72 meters (28.61 feet) in the 1988 Games in Seoul, adding two additional gold medals and a silver medal to his collection. Lewis had the top four leaps in the competition, and his Olympic gold medal was only the latest in a lengthy series of long jump successes that spanned the 1980s. Following the disqualification of Canadian Ben Johnson, who had set a world record in the 100-meter dash (9.79 seconds), three days later for testing positive for anabolic drugs, Lewis earned his second gold medal at the 1988 Games in the 100-meter dash (9.92 seconds). Lewis was content with a silver medal in the 200-meter event.

With a leap of 8.67 meters (28.44 feet), Lewis won his third straight long-jump championship in the 1992 Olympics in Barcelona, Spain, in addition to his two further gold medals. As the U.S. 4 × 100-meter relay team achieved a world and Olympic record of 37.40 seconds, Lewis, once again serving as the team's anchor, earned his eighth gold medal. Lewis "ran through" his first jump and recorded a lackluster 8.14 meters (26.71 feet) on his second jump in the 1996 Olympics in Atlanta, Georgia, when he unexpectedly qualified for the long jump event despite being 35 years old. Lewis won his seventh gold medal with a third jump of 8.5 meters (27.89 feet), which was significantly behind any records or personal bests but still qualified as the top jump. With this, he became the most decorated American track and field Olympian with ten medals; Allyson Felix would eventually overtake him in 2021. As of 1997, Lewis had hung up his spikes for good. The International Olympic Committee recognized him as the Sportsman of the Century two years down the road.

A prolific actor, Lewis played himself in a number of films and TV shows. He started the fitness-focused Carl Lewis Foundation in 2001 and was engaged with other organizations as well. Lewis, a Democrat, declared his candidacy for the New Jersey state senate in 2011. Lewis withdrew from the contest in September when his candidacy was challenged over the state's residency requirement.

20

NADIA COMĂNECI (GYMNASTICS)

Nadia Comăneci, a Romanian gymnast, was the first gymnast to ever get a perfect score of ten in an Olympic competition. She was born on November 12, 1961, in Gheorghe Gheorghiu-Dej, which is today known as Onești, Romania.

Although Comăneci was only six years old at the time, she was found by Bela Karolyi, who would eventually become the Romanian gymnastics coach. She made her debut in the national junior championships in 1969, when she finished thirteenth. In 1970, she triumphed over the competition and took home the title. She was the all-around junior champion in 1973 and 1974, and she won three gold medals in her first international competition, which was a pre-Olympic junior meet for the nations that were part of the communist bloc. Her first international competition was in 1972. In 1975, when she competed for the first time as a senior in an international competition, she triumphed against the Russian Lyudmila Turishcheva, who had previously won five European championships. She brought home four gold medals and one silver medal. In 1976, she became the first woman to accomplish a backward double salto as a dismount from the uneven parallel bars, which allowed her to emerge victorious in the American Cup competition held in New York City.

Comăneci won the gold medals in the balance beam, the uneven bars, and the all-around individual competition at the 1976 Olympic Games held in Montreal. She scored seven perfect points and won the competition. A bronze medal was awarded to her for the floor exercises, and she was awarded a silver medal for her participation in the team. Following the conclusion of the 1976 Games, her nation honored her by selecting her as a Hero of Socialist Labor. After being renamed "Nadia's Theme (The Young and the Restless)," the tune that was originally used to accompany her floor workouts went on to become a worldwide phenomenon and was awarded a Grammy Award in 1977. Her performance in the world championships in 1978 was less than satisfactory, as she ended in fourth place. Furthermore, she was unable to compete for most of 1979 due to an infection in her hand. She ended up tied for first place in the floor exercises competition at the 1980 Olympic Games held in Moscow with Nelli Kim of the Soviet Union. She won gold medals in both the beam and floor exercises competitions. As a part of her team, she was awarded a silver medal, and in the all-around individual competition, she tied with Maxi Gnauck of East Germany for second place. In 1984, she put an end to her career as a rival.

Comăneci fled to the United States of America in 1989, and she gained citizenship in the United States in 2001. She tied the knot with the American gymnast Bart Conner in 1996, and the two of them went on to collaborate on various projects to promote gymnastics. She has written two books: the autobiography Nadia (1981) and the book Letters to a Young Gymnast (2003), which is about mentoring young gymnasts. When Comăneci was admitted into the International Gymnastics Hall of Fame in 1993, she was the second person to be honored with this honor, after Olga Korbut.

21

MICHAEL SCHUMACHER (FORMULA 1)

Michael Schumacher is a German racing car driver who was born on January 3, 1969, in Hurth-Hermulhein, West Germany (now in Germany). He is known for setting records for the most Formula One (F1) Grand Prix race wins (91, which were subsequently broken by Lewis Hamilton) and F1 series titles (seven, which were later equaled by Hamilton).

The fact that Schumacher's father managed a go-kart track helped Schumacher develop an interest in go-kart racing when he was a young boy. This passion was backed by Schumacher's father. He won the German junior karting championship in 1984 and 1985, and then in 1987, he won both the German and European karting crowns. He was a winner in both of these categories. The next year, when he was 19 years old, he decided to walk away from karting and start driving Formula Three (F3) cars, which were vehicles that were less powerful than the Formula One racers. The next year, in 1990, he triumphed in the German Formula Three championship.

In 1991, Schumacher made the transition to Formula One racing by joining the Jordan team as a driver. The next year, he made the transition to Benetton, and he went on to win the driver's world championship title with that team in both 1994 and 1995. He made the transition to the Ferrari team before the 1996 season, and he ended up finishing third in the championship standings of that year. In 1999, Schumacher was involved in a collision that resulted in a damaged leg. However, he was able to recover and ultimately win a third championship the following year. This was Ferrari's first driver's crown since 1979. The victory he achieved in 2000 was the first in a series of five consecutive world championships that he won between 2000 and 2004. His grand total of seven Formula One titles eclipsed the record of five that Juan Manuel Fangio had held for almost half a century. When it came to Formula One standings, he finished in third place in 2005 and second place in 2006, respectively.

In order to continue working for Ferrari as a test driver and advisor, Schumacher decided to retire at the conclusion of the 2006 season. The previous record for most Formula One Grand Prix race wins was held by the French driver Alain Prost, who had 51 triumphs at the time of his retirement. He had 91 victories at the time of his retirement. Schumacher made the announcement in December 2009 that he would be returning to Formula One for the 2010 season as a driver for the Mercedes team of Formula One. During his return, he competed for Mercedes for three seasons, although he never won a race and never placed higher than ninth in the overall Formula One standings. In 2012, he resigned once again from the sport.

Despite the fact that Schumacher had exceptional success on the track, he was also one of the highest-paid sportsmen in the history of sports. This was accomplished via a mix of winner's purses and sponsorships. At the height of his career, it was reported that he brought in a hundred million dollars a year. Additionally, Schumacher was well-known for his extensive humanitarian work. He was given the title of special ambassador for UNESCO in 2002, and he made news for his gift of ten million dollars to the relief effort for the tsunami that occurred in the Indian Ocean in 2004.

In December 2013, Schumacher was skiing in France when he fell and struck his head on a rock. In spite of the fact that he was wearing a helmet at the time of the accident, he suffered major brain damage and was put in a coma at the request of medical professionals until June of the following year.

22

TOM BRADY (AMERICAN FOOTBALL)

American football quarterback Tom Brady was born on August 3, 1977, in San Mateo, California. He has a record seven Super Bowl triumphs with different teams (2002), five in 2005, one in 2017, one in 2019, and one in 2021. Brady was awarded MVP of the game five times (2002), in addition to his other accomplishments.

Brady often went to San Francisco 49ers games in the 1980s to see Joe Montana play quarterback. Montana was Brady's hero and someone he would come to be compared to. Brady was a high school baseball and football star. He went into the 1995 MLB draft with the Montreal Expos as a first-round choice, but he chose to play football at Michigan instead. Brady, who did not make his college football debut until his sophomore year, was known as a tough and smart player without much athletic ability, yet he helped Michigan win the 1999 Orange Bowl. He put in a lot of time and effort during his first year to become stronger and develop better technique after the New England Patriots selected him in the sixth round of the 2000 NFL draft.

Brady was selected to replace injured Patriots starting quarterback Drew Bledsoe in the 2001 season's second game. His performance was average at best, but he was reliable, sticking to basic moves and making few errors. The Patriots were 11-3 during the regular season with Brady as quarterback and went on to defeat the St. Louis Rams in Super Bowl XXXVI; Brady was awarded MVP of the game. With Brady at the helm for the first three seasons, the Patriots went 40-12, solidifying their place among the league's finest teams. Brady won his second Super Bowl MVP trophy in 2004 as the Patriots made a triumphant return to the big game, this time beating the Panthers of Carolina. The next year, riding on their success, the Patriots broke the record established by the 1972–73 Miami Dolphins with a 21–game winning run. At the end of the season, Brady and the Patriots defeated the Philadelphia Eagles in the Super Bowl for the third time in four years.

New England had the first 16-0 regular season in NFL history under Brady's leadership in 2007, and he was named NFL MVP for his record-setting 50 touchdown passes (broken in 2013 by Brady's old nemesis Peyton Manning). But in Super Bowl XLII, the underdog New York Giants defeated the Patriots. Brady tore his ACL in the 2008 season opener and had to have surgery to terminate his season. After a one-year slump, he led the Patriots to the postseason the next year and was named to the Pro Bowl. While leading the Patriots to a 14-2 record in 2010, Brady threw for 36 touchdowns, which was the most in the NFL that season. He became the only player in league history to win the MVP award twice, even though the Patriots lost their first playoff game the following season.

While leading the Patriots to another Super Bowl defeat at the hands of the Giants in February 2012, Brady passed for 5,235 yards in the 2011 season, making him one of two quarterbacks to do so (the other being Drew Brees). This record had been held by Dan Marino and was later surpassed by Manning in 2013. In 2012 and 2013, Brady guided the Patriots to defeats in the AFC title games while maintaining his Pro Bowl level of performance. After a disappointing regular season in 2014, Brady set a new record with his record-setting sixth Super Bowl start as quarterback, leading the Patriots to an AFC title game victory against the Indianapolis Colts. The Patriots' triumph was quickly overshadowed by controversy, however, when it came to light that eleven of the twelve footballs used in the game were significantly underinflated. This makes them easier to handle and throw further. Brady rallied the Patriots to a 28-24 victory against the Seahawks in the fourth quarter while the NFL investigated the event, which became known as "Deflategate," but the league did not take any action before the Super Bowl. In the game, Brady threw for 328 yards and four touchdowns, earning his third Super Bowl MVP award.

23

KOBE BRYANT (BASKETBALL)

American professional basketball player Kobe Bryant was born on August 23, 1978, in Philadelphia, Pennsylvania, U.S. He passed away on January 26, 2020, in Calabasas, California. Bryant was a key member of the Los Angeles Lakers' championship teams in 2000–02 and 2009–10.

Joe ("Jelly Bean") Bryant, whom Bryant attended school with, was a professional basketball player. He played for eight years in the National Basketball Association and another eight in Italy. Upon his family's return to the US, Bryant continued his basketball career at Lower Merion High School in Ardmore, Pennsylvania. While there, he surpassed Wilt Chamberlain's record for scoring in southeastern Pennsylvania with 2,883 points and won many national Player of the Year honors. Bryant entered the NBA draft upon graduating from high school, opting not to attend college. With the thirteenth overall selection in the 1996 NBA Draft, the Charlotte Hornets selected him. Not long after being moved to the Lakers, he became the second-youngest player in NBA history when the 1996–97 season began. After just two seasons with the Lakers, he became the league's youngest-ever All-Star after swiftly establishing his worth.

Because of the popularity and skill of his Lakers colleague Shaquille O'Neal, Bryant was compelled to share the position of star player. Despite their tense dynamic, the Lakers' success stemmed from Phil Jackson's direction once he took over as coach in 1999. At the age of 23, the Lakers had already won three straight NBA titles because of the exceptional chemistry between shooting guard Kobe Bryant and center Shaquille O'Neal.

Bryant scored more points than any other player in the NBA in 2005–06 and 2006–07, and he won his first MVP award in 2008. Bryant averaged an incredible 32.4 points per game in the 2009 NBA Finals, helping him win his fourth championship and earning him the title of most valuable Player. The 2009–10 season was the third consecutive year that he captained the Lakers to the Western Conference title, and he was again selected as the NBA finals MVP after the team's seven-game victory against the Boston Celtics. The next three seasons saw the Lakers win their division, but they never made it beyond the second round of the playoffs. With superstars Steve Nash and Dwight Howard joining the Lakers' roster in 2012–13, the team was heavily favored to win the NBA title. However, after a disappointing season, the team was in danger of missing the playoffs altogether when Bryant tore his Achilles tendon in April 2013, ending his season prematurely. The Lakers were eliminated in the first round of the playoffs that season, finishing as the eighth and last seed. He got back on the court in December 2013, but he only got to play in six games before he hurt his kneecap and had to sit out the rest of the season. After making a brief comeback at the start of the 2014–15 season, Bryant had a setback in January 2015 when he tore his rotator cuff. He returned for most of the 2015–16 season but once again had a rough go of it, shooting a career-low. 358 with 17.6 ppg. He finally called it quits after the last regular-season game of the season.

24

RAFAEL NADAL (TENNIS)

Spanish tennis player Rafael Nadal came into his own in the new millennium, notably on clay courts, after being born on June 3, 1986, in Manacor, Mallorca, Spain. He became the first player in Grand Slam men's singles history to win 22 titles, and he won 14 French Open championships in his career.

As a child, Nadal was immersed in the world of sports; his uncle, Miguel Angel Nadal, played professional association football (soccer) and was a World Cup competitor in 2002. Toni Nadal, Rafael's second uncle, gave him tennis lessons when he was four years old and continued to teach him on the professional circuit. Nadal used to play left-handed tennis with a two-handed forehand and backhand when he was younger, even though he wrote with his right hand. But his uncle pushed for him to switch to a more traditional left-handed grip when he was twelve years old. The one-handed forehand that would become Nadal's trademark helped propel him to the pinnacle of tennis, but he continued to use his two-handed backhand.

Even though he became a professional in 2001, Nadal had competed in only one Grand Slam event as a junior, making it to the semifinals of the 2002 Wimbledon Championships. The next year, he launched his career seriously, eventually becoming one of the world's top 50. When Spain beat the US in the Davis Cup final in 2004, he was an integral part of the victory. Nadal became the youngest player in the history of the international team tournament to win a singles match for a successful country, topping Andy Roddick—then the number two in the world—in a four-set opening-day singles showdown. Nadal was 18 years and six months old.

Nadal swiftly rose to the ranks of the best players on the ATP circuit, thanks to his devastatingly powerful heavy topspin forehand and his ability to traverse the court with ease. He also became embroiled in a spat with Roger Federer, the top player in the world. When Nadal defeated Roger Federer in the quarterfinals of the 2005 French Open (Roland Garros), he became the youngest male player to win 11 tournaments. This included his debut at Roland Garros, where he achieved the record. After defeating Roger Federer in the final of the French Open the following year, Nadal went on to win five more ATP circuit championships. Also, he lost to Federer in the Wimbledon final, which was his first grass-court final.

Before Federer defeated him in the 2007 ATP Masters Series Hamburg (Germany) final on May 20, Nadal had won an unprecedented 81 straight matches on clay. Federer defeated Nadal in a punishing five-set Wimbledon final that lasted three hours and forty-five minutes after Nadal bounced back to win his third Roland Garros championship. When these two played again in the 2008 French Open final, Nadal defeated Federer to win the championship for the fourth time in a row, matching Björn Borg for most consecutive French Open victories. The 2008 Wimbledon final was the third straight meeting between Nadal and Federer. In a five-set showdown that lasted four hours and forty-eight minutes, Nadal became the first player since Borg (1980) to win the French Open and Wimbledon in the same year, adding to his Grand Slam trophy collection. The match was the longest men's singles final in Wimbledon history. Upon defeating Roger Federer to become the world number one in August 2008, Nadal went on to win the men's singles gold medal at the 2008 Beijing Olympics.

25

MAGIC JOHNSON (BASKETBALL)

The American basketball player Magic Johnson, who was born on August 14, 1959, in Lansing, Michigan, USA, won five NBA championships while playing for the Los Angeles Lakers.

Johnson, whose father was an autoworker, became known as "Magic" in high school for his entertaining and imaginative ballhandling. He was a fierce competitor who won the 1977 state title with his high school team and the 1979 NCAA title with Michigan State University, defeating Larry Bird and Indiana State in the process. Following his second year at Michigan State, Johnson departed for the Lakers, who had the first overall choice in the 1979 NBA draft and chose Johnson with that selection.

While playing professionally, Johnson was at his best, leading the Los Angeles Lakers to five NBA titles (1980, 1982, 1985, 1987, and 1988). In his rookie year, Johnson won his first championship. In the 1979–80 NBA finals, he made history by playing all five positions to help the Lakers win the championship. Johnson was also the first rookie to receive the MVP award in the NBA playoffs. In all three of those years (1987, 1989, and 1990), he was also awarded league MVP. He added fresh variety to the position of point guard when he played there. Throughout his thirteen-year career, he averaged 19.5 points and 7.2 rebounds per game, demonstrating his versatility as a scorer and rebounder at 6 feet 9 inches (2.06 meters). But his ability to make game-winning plays in the last seconds and his creative no-look and bounce passes made him famous. Competition for NBA dominance between Johnson's Lakers and Bird's Boston Celtics ushered in a golden age for the sport and its fans.

When Johnson announced his immediate retirement from basketball and his diagnosis of HIV on November 7, 1991, he stunned the basketball world and made headlines worldwide. Johnson had 9,921 assists when he first retired from the NBA; John Stockton eventually surpassed him in 1995. He got back into basketball in 1992, playing in the All-Star Game and winning Most Valuable Player honors. He also competed in the 1992 Summer Olympics in Barcelona, where he was a member of the "Dream Team" that won the men's basketball gold medal. In the years that followed, he not only played with the Lakers for part of the 1995–96 season but also briefly coached them (1994). His ownership of the franchise was in the minority from 1994 until 2010.

Johnson became a notable HIV/AIDS campaigner and a very successful entrepreneur after retiring from basketball. His investing business has estimated assets of almost $1 billion as of 2020. He was a member of the group that bought the Los Angeles Dodgers in 2012. In 2017, he made a triumphant return to the Lakers club, this time taking on the role of advisor to owner Jeanie Buss. His rapid promotion to president of basketball operations after just a few weeks put Johnson in charge of the Lakers' front office. He unexpectedly stepped down at the conclusion of the 2018–19 season, citing a lackluster stint, saying he preferred to be an ambassador for the sport. In 1996, Johnson was selected as one of the 50 all-time best players in NBA history. In 2002, he became a member of the Naismith Memorial Basketball Hall of Fame. The 2022 documentary series They Call Me Magic chronicled Johnson's life and work.

26

LARRY BIRD (BASKETBALL)

Larry Bird, a native American, was born on December 7, 1956, in West Baden, Indiana. He is widely regarded as one of the best pure shooters in NBA history and the driving force behind the three titles won by the Boston Celtics (1981, 1984, and 1986).

Originally from French Lick, Indiana, Bird attended Indiana State University, where he was a key figure in reviving the school's basketball program and guiding his final-year squad to a 33-1 record. The 1979–80 season came to a close with a defeat against Michigan State University in the NCAA championship game. That was the first encounter between Magic Johnson and Larry Bird, the man whose rivalry would become the focal point of the NBA's 1980s popularity. After Bird's junior year at Indiana State (1978), the Celtics picked him. However, he did not play professionally until the 1979–80 season. It was at this time that he earned Rookie of the Year after helping the team to one of the greatest single-season turnarounds in NBA history, a 32-win improvement.

In his thirteen years with the Celtics, the man who called himself the "hick from French Lick" solidified his place in NBA lore as a legend. A frightening presence on the court, the 6-foot-9-inch (2.06-meter) big was renowned for his unflappable confidence and clutch shooting skills. Under Bird's leadership, the Celtics won the NBA championship in 1981, their first (and 14th overall). The next two years, 1984 and 1986, they made it a hat trick. Bird became the first player from outside the center to win three straight league MVP awards (1984–1986) and was named to the All-Star team twelve times. Before he retired, he had scored 21,791 points, which was the eleventh-highest total in NBA history. He averaged 24.3 points, 10.1 rebounds, and 6.3 assists per game. Bird earned a gold medal in basketball in 1992 in Barcelona as a part of the "Dream Team," which included other NBA superstars. In 1998, he was inducted into the Naismith Memorial Basketball Hall of Fame.

After Bird's retirement in 1992, he took a job in the Celtics' front office. Despite his lack of coaching experience, he was selected as the Indiana Pacers' head coach in 1997 and went on to win the title the following season. Bird became the president of basketball operations for the Pacers in 2003 after stepping down as head coach in 2000, the year after leading the team to an NBA finals berth. Shortly after being named the Pacers' Executive of the Year the previous season, in June 2012, he decided to leave his position in the front office. He took a year off from basketball in 2012, but in June 2013, he was back with the Pacers as their head of basketball operations. After constructing teams that made it to the playoffs eight times in thirteen seasons as head coach, Bird resigned in May 2017. He then worked as a consultant and scout with the Pacers.

27

AYRTON SENNA (FORMULA 1)

Born on March 21, 1960, in São Paulo, Brazil, Ayrton Senna was a Brazilian race-car driver who achieved recognition for being a ferocious competitor. He was notorious for his ruthless and reckless tactics on the Grand Prix track. Senna passed away on May 1, 1994, in Imola, Italy. He swiftly progressed through the ranks of professional racing, winning 41 Grand Prix titles and three circuit world championships (1988, 1990, and 1991). He also won the world championship in the Formula One racing series. His life was cut tragically short when he was involved in an accident that occurred at the San Marino Grand Prix in 1994.

His father introduced him to the world of go-karting when Senna was only four years old, and it was then that Senna found his passion for racing. Senna is the son of a rich businessman and factory owner. He got his first full-size go-kart when he was ten years old, and he started racing as soon as he was legally permitted to do so, which was when he was thirteen years old. 1977 and 1978 were the years that Senna triumphed in the South American Kart Championship.

In 1981, Senna relocated to England in order to compete for the Van Diemen team using the Formula Ford 1600 level of competition. However, he departed for a short period of time at the conclusion of the season in order to join the family company. He won multiple races. On the other hand, he went back to England briefly after that in order to compete in Formula Ford 2000 there for the next season. In 1983, he made the transition to Formula Three racing, which is the second level of international Grand Prix competition. Through his participation with the West Surrey Racing Team, he was able to triumph in both the Macau Grand Prix and the national championship. In 1984, he started making his debut as a Formula One (F1) driver for Toleman. In his debut year, he finished in second place in the Monaco Grand Prix. Despite the fact that he had seized the lead after 31 laps, the race was halted due to terrible weather, and a scoring technicality put him in second position.

Senna moved to Lotus in 1985 in search of a more satisfactory automobile. During that particular year, he was victorious in both the Portuguese Grand Prix and the Circuit de Spa-Francorchamps in Belgium, and he concluded the season in fourth place overall. In 1988, he became a member of the McLaren team. Senna won a record eight races during his first season with his new team, winning his maiden Formula One title and setting a new record for the most victories to date. In 1989, he finished second behind his colleague Alain Prost, and tensions between the two caused Prost to join Ferrari following the season. This led to the beginning of a significant rivalry between the two drivers over the subsequent four years. Both in 1990 and 1991, Senna won six and seven races, respectively, and went on to win the Formula One championship in both of those years. In 1992, he came in fourth position, and in 1993, he finished in second place, with Prost coming in second. However, he closed that season on a high note by winning the last race of the year. The win would turn out to be the last one he would ever achieve in a race.

Senna suffered severe head injuries and passed away as a result of a collision with a concrete barrier that occurred at the San Marino Grand Prix in 1994. It was his Formula One career that was the focus of the documentary Senna (2010), which won several awards.

28

ROGER BANNISTER (TRACK AND FIELD)

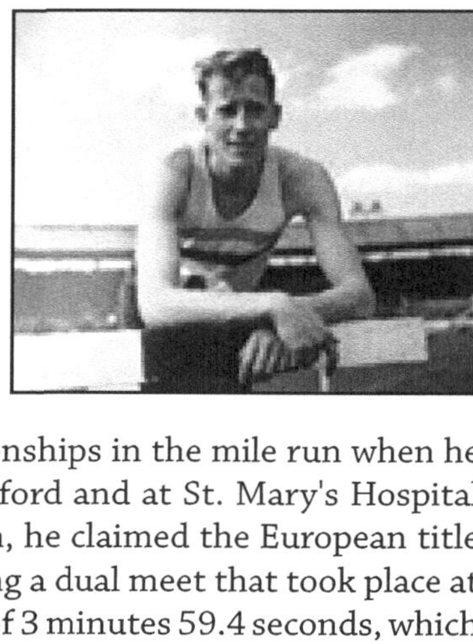

Roger Bannister was an English neurologist who was the first athlete to run a mile in less than four minutes. He was born on March 23, 1929, in Harrow, Middlesex, England, and passed away on March 3, 2018, in Oxford, Oxfordshire.

Bannister won the British (1951, 1953–54) and Empire (1954) championships in the mile run when he was a student at the University of Oxford and at St. Mary's Hospital Medical School in London. In addition, he claimed the European title in the 1,500-meter race in 1954. During a dual meet that took place at Oxford on May 6, 1954, he ran a mark of 3 minutes 59.4 seconds, which allowed him to break the four-minute barrier. His successful rejection of the "psychological" barrier, which is the widespread perception that it is impossible to run a mile in less than four minutes, was practically incidental to his achievement of breaking the world record for running a mile in less than four minutes and thirteen seconds, which had been held by Gunder Hagg of Sweden for nine years. It is stated that Bannister was able to reach his speed by using scientific training techniques and doing extensive study into the mechanics of running. In the book titled "The Four Minute Mile," which was published in 1955, he detailed his experiences.

Bannister received his medical degree from Oxford in 1963, after which he went on to become a neurologist. He graduated from St. Mary's High School in 1954. His publications included articles on the physiology of exercise, heart disease, and neurological topics. Beginning in 1969, he was the editor of Brain's Clinical Neurology, which was later renamed Brain and Bannister's Clinical Neurology, seventh edition, published in 1990. In 1975, he was awarded the title of knight.

29

BJORN BORG (TENNIS)

Bjorn Borg, a Swedish tennis player who was born on June 6, 1956, in Stockholm, Sweden, was widely considered to be among the most accomplished competitors of the contemporary age. Since Laurie Doherty (1902–06), he accomplished the feat of winning the Wimbledon singles title five years in a row (1976–80). He was the first player to accomplish this feat. In the span of 1974–1975 and 1978–1981, he achieved a remarkable feat by winning the men's singles title in the French Open for a record-breaking four consecutive years.

At a very young age, Borg began to learn how to play tennis, and by the time he was 13 years old, he was already able to defeat Sweden's most talented junior players. When Borg was just 14 years old, he made his debut on the professional tour. He went on to win the Italian Open at the age of 17 and the French Open at the age of 18. He is known for his strong serve and two-handed backhand. It was in 1975 when he was instrumental in Sweden's victory in the Davis Cup. At that point, he had already won 16 straight cup singles, surpassing Bill Tilden's record of 12 consecutive victories. Borg had won 41 singles matches and five championships in a row by the time he ultimately lost at Wimbledon to John McEnroe in the spring of 1981. This was a record that had never been established before. Borg, on the other hand, turned out to be unsuccessful in winning two of the four Grand Slam tournaments, namely the United States Open and the Australian Open.

Borg made a sudden announcement in January 1983 that he was retiring from the professional tennis circuit. However, he did make an effort to return in 1991, although it was only temporary. When Borg was in his early twenties, he established a prosperous sportswear firm. In 1980, he collaborated with Eugene Scott to write the book "Bjorn Borg: My Life and Game." Borg was acknowledged by the International Tennis Hall of Fame with his induction in the year 1987.

30

MARTINA HINGIS (TENNIS)

The Swiss professional tennis player Martina Hingis became the youngest individual in the "open" period to win a Grand Slam singles title and the youngest to be named world number one. She was born on September 30, 1980, in Košice, Czechoslovakia, which is now in Slovakia. She won five Grand Slam singles tournaments throughout her brief and injury-marred career: the Australian Open (1997, 1998, 1999), Wimbledon (1997), and the US Open (1997).

Martina Navratilova inspired Hingis's name. Melanie Molitor, a former Czechoslovakian tennis star, and Karol Hingis, a tennis coach, were her parents' primary sports role models. After learning to ski and play tennis at the age of three, the younger Hingis started competing in tennis events when she was five years old. At the age of seven, she and her mother relocated to Trübbach, Switzerland, after her parents' divorce. Soon after, Molitor started instructing her daughter Hingis tennis vigorously, and the little player made quick progress. She won the 1993 junior French Open at the tender age of twelve, making her the youngest person to ever win a Grand Slam junior title. A few weeks after becoming the youngest junior Wimbledon winner in 1994, Hingis won again in France.

Shortly after turning fourteen years old in October 1994, Hingis began competing professionally. Three months after she reached the second round of the 1995 Australian Open, she became the youngest player to ever win a match in a Grand Slam tournament. In 1996, Hingis became the youngest player in Wimbledon history to win the doubles event, partnering with Helena Sukova. However, many were critical of Hingis for becoming professional at such a young age. Shortly after she made her professional debut, the Women's Tennis Association (WTA) implemented new regulations that restricted the number of tournaments open to players aged 15–17 and outright banned players aged 14 from participating in regular tour events.

After starting the year 1997 at #4 in the world, Hingis went on to win six consecutive events, including the Australian Open. After Lottie Dod won Wimbledon in 1887 at the age of 15, she became the second youngest player ever to win a Grand Slam; with that triumph, she was sixteen years old. Similarly, Hingis rose to the top spot that year. Hingis defeated opponents with a varied variety of strokes and clever play rather than her might. After losing to Iva Majoli in the French Open final, she went on to win Wimbledon and the US Open, resuming her winning run. She went on to win the Australian Open in 1998 and 1999 and have other Grand Slam event final appearances in the years that followed. She got all the way to the finals of the 2002 Australian Open despite having ankle surgery in 2001; Jennifer Capriati ended up beating her.

In 2003, Hingis retired due to a series of ailments. But she made a triumphant comeback to the WTA two years down the road. Her success was curbed by injuries and the emergence of formidable opponents, most notably the Williams sisters, Venus and Serena. After releasing her cocaine test result at Wimbledon in 2007, Hingis resigned from competitive tennis. A two-year suspension was imposed on her, notwithstanding her denial of drug use. She won a total of 43 singles championships and 10 Grand Slam doubles championships, including both mixed and women's events. Also, she had been at the top for 209 weeks, but they weren't consecutive. Then, Hingis started competing in events for seniors.

The International Tennis Hall of Fame honored Hingis with an induction in 2013. She rejoined the WTA later that year and began competing in doubles tournaments. In 2017, she retired for the third time after winning an extra ten Grand Slam doubles championships.

31

JERRY RICE (AMERICAN FOOTBALl)

Jerry Rice is a professional gridiron football player from the United States. He was born on October 13, 1962, in Starkville, Mississippi, and many people believe him to be the best wide receiver in the history of the National Football League (NFL). He established a number of National Football League records when he was mostly playing with the San Francisco 49ers. These marks include those for career touchdowns (208), catches (1,549), and receiving yards (22,895).

Rice, who was the son of a brick mason, was renowned for having grown strong and dependable hands via the process of collecting bricks that his siblings tossed to him while they were working for their father. For the purpose of receiving a football scholarship, he attended Mississippi Valley State University in Itta Bena. Not only did he receive All-America honors, but he also established 18 records in Division I-AA of the National Collegiate Athletic Association, including the record for the most receptions in a single game, which he accomplished with 24.

Following the first round of the 1985 National Football League draft, Rice was selected by the San Francisco 49ers. In the beginning, he had a hard time keeping the ball in his possession since he was concentrating on the complex throw patterns of the San Francisco system. However, during his second season, he was able to catch 86 passes and lead the league in receiving yards (1,570) and touchdown receptions (15). Rice was able to flourish in the "West Coast" strategy that was implemented by San Francisco head coach Bill Walsh. This approach was characterized by a high volume of short, rapid throws from the quarterback and accurate route running by the receivers. In 1987, he was voted the NFL Player of the Year and established a record for the most touchdown catches in a single season with twenty-two. This was accomplished despite the fact that a players' strike restricted the season to twelve games. Rice was taller than the average wide receiver in the National Football League, at 6 feet 2 inches (1.9 meters) tall. He used his height and power to outmatch opponents with his athleticism. In addition to that, he was an outstanding runner after landing a catch.

Rice, along with quarterback Joe Montana and defensive back Ronnie Lott, became nearly associated with the 49ers. He was a member of three Super Bowl championship teams with the 49ers, including the squad that won the title in 1988, 1989, and 1994. He was honored with the title of Most Valuable Player for the 1988 season of Super Bowl XXIII, and he established a number of records for the Super Bowl. Rice was selected for the Pro Bowl on a yearly basis from 1986 through 1998. Rice was moved to the Oakland Raiders before the 2001 season by the San Francisco 49ers, which was a contentious decision that was made in order to develop younger players. In the next season, he contributed to the Raiders' advancement to Super Bowl XXXVII, where they were ultimately beaten by the Tampa Bay Buccaneers. During that season, he became the first player in NFL history to record more than 200 touchdowns in his career. In 2003, he participated in the Pro Bowl for the thirteenth time. Rice was traded to the Seattle Seahawks in the middle of the 2004 season; however, after the conclusion of the season, the Seahawks decided to remove him from their roster. The next year, he made an unsuccessful effort to become a starting receiver with the Denver Broncos. As a result, he signed a ceremonial one-day contract with San Francisco and retired from the 49ers. In the year 2010, Rice was honored with induction into the Pro Football Hall of Fame.

32

KAREEM ABDUL-JABBAR (BASKETBALL)

Kareem Abdul-Jabbar was an American basketball player who played at the college and professional levels. He was a powerful center who stood 7 feet 2 inches (2.18 meters) tall and dominated the game during the 1970s and early 1980s. Abdul-Jabbar was born on April 16, 1947, in New York, New York, United States.

Abdul-Jabbar brought a superb shooting touch to the position and a broad variety of beautiful post moves, notably his sweeping, virtually indefensible sky hook. Despite the fact that he lacked the physical power of NBA centers Chamberlain and Willis Reed, Abdul-Jabbar was able to bring these qualities to the position. He was also an exceptional ball passer. After receiving the NBA Most Valuable Player award a record six times, Kareem Abdul-Jabbar decided to go into retirement at the conclusion of the 1988–1989 season. After an exceptionally lengthy career, he had established records in the National Basketball Association (NBA) for the most points scored (38,387; subsequently broken by LeBron James), the most field goals made (15,837), and the most minutes played (57,446) among all players. At the time of his retirement, Kareem Abdul-Jabbar had also gathered the third most career rebounds (17,440) and the most blocked shots in the history of the league (3,189; this record has since been surpassed by Hakeem Olajuwon and Dikembe Mutombo). In 1996, he was recognized as one of the 50 best players in the history of the National Basketball Association (NBA), and he was inducted into the Naismith Memorial Basketball Hall of Fame in 1995.

In his spare time, Abdul-Jabbar followed his hobbies of acting and writing in addition to his basketball career. He had appearances on television as well as in a few films, perhaps the most notable of which was his performance as a copilot in the comedy picture Airplane! (1980). Giant Steps, his autobiography, was released to the public in the year 1983. His writings on the African American experience also included Black Profiles in Courage: A Legacy of African-American Achievement (1996; with Alan Steinberg), Brothers in Arms: The Epic Story of the 761st Tank Battalion, WWII's Forgotten Heroes (2004; with Anthony Walton), On the Shoulders of Giants: My Personal Journey Through the Harlem Renaissance (2007; with Raymond Obstfeld), and the children's book What Color Is My World?: The Lost History of African-American Inventors (2012; with Obstfeld). In addition, he is the author of Coach Wooden and Me: Our 50-Year Friendship on and off the Court (2017), as well as a mystery trilogy featuring Sherlock Holmes's elder brother, Mycroft: Mycroft Holmes (2015), Mycroft and Sherlock (2018), and Mycroft and Sherlock: The Empty Birdcage (2019). This book was written in collaboration with Anna Waterhouse. In addition to his coaching and consulting work in basketball, Abdul-Jabbar also spent some time working on the White Mountain Apache Reservation in Arizona. The Presidential Medal of Freedom was bestowed to him one year ago, in 2016.

33

STEFFI GRAF (TENNIS)

During the late 1980s and 1990s, German tennis star Steffi Graf dominated women's tennis by winning 22 Grand Slam singles championships. Graf was born on June 14, 1969, in Brühl, West Germany, which is now located in Germany.

The support that Graf received from her father, who eventually became her coach, led her to begin playing tennis. At the age of thirteen, she achieved the distinction of being the second youngest player in the history of global rankings. She won her first Grand Slam competition in 1987 when she triumphed against Martina Navratilova, an American who was born in the Czech Republic, at the French Open. The year 1988 was the year when she became the third woman to win all four Grand Slam events in a single calendar year. These tournaments were the Australian Open, the French Open, Wimbledon, and the United States Open. Additionally, she earned a gold medal at the Olympic Games in Seoul, which was an extraordinary accomplishment that became known as the "Golden Slam."

As Churandy Martina (left) of the Netherlands Antilles and Brian Dzingai of Zimbabwe come in after him in the Men's 200-meter Final at the National Stadium during Day 12 of the Beijing 2008 Olympic Games on August 20, 2008, in Beijing, China, Usain Bolt of Jamaica reacts after breaking the world record with a time of 19.30 seconds to win the gold medal. The event took place on August 20, 2008 in Beijing, China.

Graf was renowned for her intensity, speed, and powerful forehand, and by the 1990s, she had established herself as one of the most accomplished players in the world. She had won multiple singles titles at the French Open (1987–88, 1993, 1995–96, and 1999), the Australian Open (1988–90 and 1994), and the United States Open (1988–89, 1993, and 1995–96). After Navratilova's nine triumphs in the open period, she had seven victories at Wimbledon (1988–89, 1991–93, and 1995–96). Her seven victories were the second most in the open era. Graf, who had been troubled by ailments throughout his career, decided to retire from the sport shortly after losing in the finals of Wimbledon in the year 1999.

The public spotlight continued to follow Graf even after she retired from her position. In 2001, she tied the knot with another tennis great, Andre Agassi, and the duo became active in a number of philanthropic causes. One of these causes was Children for Tomorrow, which Graf had established in 1998 as a non-profit organization with the purpose of providing assistance to children and families who were devastated by war and other calamities. During the year 2004, Graf was honored with induction into the International Tennis Hall of Fame.

34

MIKE TYSON (BOXING)

Born on June 30, 1966, in Brooklyn, New York, USA, American boxer Mike Tyson became the youngest heavyweight champion in history when he was twenty years old.

Tyson was sent to a reform school in upstate New York in 1978 after being a part of many street gangs since he was a young boy. Bobby Stewart, a social worker and boxing fan, saw his talent in the reform school and put him in touch with the famous trainer Cus D'Amato, who later became his legal guardian. Before becoming professional in 1985, Tyson had an impressive amateur record of 24-3.

D'Amato instructed Tyson in the peekaboo boxing technique, which rendered his defense almost impenetrable—a combination of keeping his hands close to his cheeks and engaging in a continual bobbing motion while in the ring. Even though Tyson didn't seem like a traditional heavyweight boxer—all 5 feet, 11 inches (1.8 meters) and approximately 218 pounds (99 kg)—he surprised everyone with his lightning speed and aggression on the mat. After knocking out Trevor Berbick in the second round on November 22, 1986, he became the youngest heavyweight champion in World Boxing Council (WBC) history. He won the World Boxing Association (WBA) title on March 7, 1987, by defeating James Smith. The three sanctioning bodies—the World Boxing Council (WBC), the World Boxing Association (WBA), and the International Boxing Federation [IBF]—unanimously acknowledged Tyson as champion after his August 1, 1987, victory against Tony Tucker.

Tyson allied with contentious promoter Don King after the demise of D'Amato and manager Jimmy Jacobs. Among his ten successful championship defenses was a win against Michael Spinks and Larry Holmes, two former heavyweight champions. Actress Robin Givens was Tyson's spouse in 1988, but the pair filed for a divorce in 1989 after she accused Tyson of physical abuse. As a result, Tyson was later the target of several harassment and assault allegations.

James ("Buster") Douglas, who was little respected, defeated Tyson for the belt with a technical knockout in the tenth round on February 11, 1990, in a shocking turn of events in boxing history. Following that setback, Tyson won four in a row. On the other hand, he was found guilty in 1992 of raping a beauty pageant competitor in 1991.

In 1996, after serving his sentence, Tyson returned to boxing and easily defeated Frank Bruno and Bruce Seldon to reclaim two of his championship titles. A technical knockout in the eleventh round ended Tyson's second professional loss on November 9, 1996, in a highly anticipated fight against two-time heavyweight champion Evander Holyfield. He bit Holyfield's ears twice in their rematch on June 28, 1997, which led to his disqualification and the loss of his boxing license.

After getting his boxing license reinstated, Tyson made a triumphant comeback to the ring on January 16, 1999, scoring a fifth-round knockout victory against Franz Botha. After pleading no contest to charges of assaulting two elderly men after a 1998 vehicle accident, Tyson received a year in prison, two years of probation, 200 hours of community service, and a fine of $2,500 on February 6. After just a few months after completing his one-year term, Tyson was freed.

The issues with self-control that Tyson had persisted, however. In June of 2000, when the referee intervened in a fight between American Lou Savarese and Tyson, the latter continued to hit, accidentally hurting the referee. After the fight, Tyson spoke to the press and made some strange and nasty statements about British heavyweight champion Lennox Lewis, which angered boxing fans. With a third-round victory against Andrew Golota in October 2000, Tyson's subsequent failed drug test led to the fight's subsequent declaration of a no-contest. Prior to his bout with Lewis in June 2002, Tyson fought only once more between October 2000 and that date.

35

WILT CHAMBERLAIN (BASKETBALL)

Wilt Chamberlain was a professional basketball player who was born on August 21, 1936, in Philadelphia, Pennsylvania, United States, and passed away on October 12, 1999, in Los Angeles, California. He is widely regarded as one of the most outstanding offensive players in the history of the game. The great center was Chamberlain, who stood at a height of more than 7 feet (2.1 measurements). It was during his 1961–1962 season that he made history by being the first player in the history of the National Basketball Association (NBA) to score more than 4,000 points in a single season. He finished with 4,029 points, averaging 50.4 points per game.

Chamberlain's performance at Overbrook High School in Philadelphia garnered him interest from more than one hundred schools and institutions while he was still a teenager. Following his time spent playing basketball at the University of Kansas for two years (1956–58), he went on to play with the Harlem Globetrotters for one year (1958–59). In 1959, he entered the National Basketball Association (NBA), where he played for the Philadelphia Warriors from

1959 until 1965 (the club relocated and renamed the San Francisco Warriors in 1962). He then returned to Philadelphia to play for the Philadelphia 76ers from 1965 until 1968, and he finished his career with the Los Angeles Lakers from 1968 to 1973. Chamberlain and Bill Russell, both of whom played for the Boston Celtics, had a long-standing rivalry that was characterized by a friendly rivalry. Many people believe that the excitement that was produced around games starring these two players is responsible for the rise in popularity of professional basketball.

Chamberlain held the record for most points scored in the National Basketball Association (NBA) until 1984 when Kareem Abdul-Jabbar broke his mark. Chamberlain's total of 31,419 points scored throughout his professional career was the most in NBA history. A career average of 30.1 points per game, which was an NBA record until it was broken by Michael Jordan, and a lifetime average of 22.9 rebounds per game are two further career highlights that Chamberlain achieved during his time in the National Basketball Association. It is true that Chamberlain has the top four single-season scoring averages in the history of the league. Among them is his NBA record of 50.4 points per game, which he achieved in the 1961–62 season. The other three records were achieved during the 1962–63 season (44.8 points per game), the 1960–61 season (38.3 points per game), and the 1959–60 season (37.6 points per game). With his 100 points scored against the New York Knicks on March 2, 1962, in Hershey, Pennsylvania, he continues to hold the record for the most points scored in a single game in the history of professional basketball. On top of that, he scored at least 56 points. Sixty-one times during the regular season, they scored 36 field goals in a single game (this occurred on March 2, 1962) and grabbed 55 rebounds in a single game (this occurred on November 24, 1960). Having never been fouled out of an NBA game was the accomplishment that Chamberlain was most proud of. In the year 1978, he was selected to be a member of the Naismith Memorial Basketball Hall of Fame.

The year 1973 saw the publication of his autobiography, which was authored in collaboration with David Shaw and titled Wilt: Just Like Any Other 7-Foot Black Millionaire Who Lives Next Door. Additionally, in 1991, Chamberlain wrote a book titled "A View from Above," which was a more in-depth revelation of his personal life.

36

JACKIE JOYNER-KERSEE (TRACK AND FIELD)

American athlete Jackie Joyner-Kersee was born on March 3, 1962, in East St. Louis, Illinois, USA. She is widely regarded as the best female athlete of all time. She set a new record in the heptathlon by scoring over 7,000 points.

Joyner has a lifelong passion for sports, and she won the National Junior Pentathlon title in her adolescent years. As a dedicated student and athlete in high school, she excelled academically and participated on many sports teams, including track, basketball, and volleyball. She graduated near the top of her class. With a leap of 6.68 meters (20 feet 7.5 inches), she became the first female Illinois high school athlete to hold that record while she was a junior. After dominating her high school track and field events, she earned a basketball and long jump scholarship at UCLA.

While Joyner was married to Bob Kersee in 1986, he was an assistant track coach, and they started preparing for the heptathlon in 1981. Despite suffering from a strained hamstring, she managed to win silver in the heptathlon at the 1984 Summer Olympics in Los Angeles, only missing out on the gold by five points. Joyner-Kersee ultimately broke through as the top heptathlete on July 7, 1986, after graduating from UCLA in 1985. At the Goodwill Games in Moscow, she established a new world record of 7,148 points. She became the first heptathlete to reach 7,000 points when her score surpassed the previous record by 202 points. In 1988, while competing for and winning the gold medal in the heptathlon at the Seoul Olympics, Joyner-Kersee established a new world record of 7,291 meters. She broke the record for most straight Olympic heptathlon wins in 1992 in Barcelona. At the 1996 Atlanta Olympics, her last competition before retiring, she won bronze in the long jump but did not compete in the heptathlon due to a hamstring injury.

In the heptathlon, Joyner-Kersee excelled in the long jump, 100-meter hurdles, 200-meter run, and high jump. She often participated in individual events, most notably the long jump, where she equaled the record in 1987 at 7.45 meters [24 feet 5.5 inches], and went on to win the gold medal in 1988 and the bronze medal in 1992. Joyner-Kersee competed in the long jump indoors after playing professional basketball for the Richmond Rage during the 1996 Olympics. She departed the team halfway through her first season. She attempted to participate in her fifth Olympic Games in 2000, but she could not make it beyond the qualifying round in the United States. That year, she formally hung up her boots.

Joyner-Kersee was active with a number of nonprofits. The Jackie Joyner-Kersee Foundation was formed in 1988 by her to aid disadvantaged children, particularly those residing in East St. Louis, Illinois, her birthplace. She went on to co-found Athletes for Hope in 2007, an organization that pushed for elite athletes to become involved in charity work. Among other things, she got engaged with a Comcast-backed programmed in 2016 to help low-income families get Internet connections. With co-author Sonja Steptoe, Joyner-Kersee released her autobiography in 1997 titled A Kind of Grace: The Autobiography of the World's Greatest Female Athlete.

37

SUGAR RAY LEONARD (BOXING)

Sugar Ray Leonard is a well-known American boxer who was born on May 17, 1956, in Rocky Mount, North Carolina, United States. He is well regarded for his agility and grace, and he won 36 of his 40 professional contests in addition to a number of trophies. He competed in the light-welterweight division in the 1976 Olympic Games in Montreal, where he won the gold medal. He was an amateur at the time.

Leonard showed his prowess as a boxer by the time he was in his mid-teens. During his amateur career, he won 145 of 150 matches, won two National Golden Glove championships (1973 and 1974), won two Amateur Athletic Union championships (1974 and 1975), and earned a gold medal in the Pan American Games in 1975. Following his triumph in the Olympic Games in 1976, he made the announcement that he would be retiring from the sport. However, on February 5, 1977, he returned to the ring as a professional.

Wilfred Benítez, the incumbent World Boxing Council (WBC) welterweight champion, was upset by Leonard in November 1979.

However, Leonard was unsuccessful in his attempt to retain the championship in June 1980, when he faced Roberto Durán in a battle that became renowned. Five months later, Leonard was able to reclaim the championship thanks to his victory against Durán. Subsequently, he was able to successfully defend the belt, and in 1981, he won the World Boxing Association (WBA) version of the title by beating Thomas Hearns. Ayub Kalule was knocked out in the ninth round, which allowed him to win the WBA junior-middleweight championship in the same year.

In 1982 and 1984, Leonard withdrew from prizefighting. However, in April 1987, he was lured to return to the sport in order to compete against the up-and-coming Marvelous Marvin Hagler. In what is widely regarded as one of the most memorable professional boxing battles in history, Leonard beat Hagler to win the WBC middleweight championship.

After suffering a defeat in a fight for the WBC super welterweight championship in 1991, Leonard once again withdrew from the sport. However, he made a comeback in 1997, when he was forty years old, and he was defeated by a technical knockout in the fifth round. As a result of the battle, he decided to retire with a record of 36 victories (25 of which were knockouts), three defeats, and one tie. The International Boxing Hall of Fame honored him with an induction ceremony later that year, in 1997. Following the conclusion of his career as a boxer, Leonard went on to become an analyst and presenter on television programming. In his autobiography, titled The Big Fight: My Life in and Out of the Ring, which was published in 2011 and was written in collaboration with Michael Arkush, Leonard discusses his difficulties with substance addiction and alcoholism, and he also claims that he was sexually molested by an "Olympic boxing coach."

38

GREG LEMOND (CYCLING)

Greg LeMond is the only cyclist from outside of Europe to ever win the Tour de France, the most prestigious and difficult race in cycling. He was born on June 26, 1961, in Lakewood, California. Three times (1986, 1989, and 1990) he triumphed in the Tour de France, and twice (1983, 1989) he won the World Road Race Championship.

Originally taking up cycling in the summertime as a means to stay active, LeMond was a passionate skier in Nevada when he was a youngster. But his cycling prowess was plain to see, and he quickly entered junior competitions. After the US decided to boycott the 1980 Moscow Olympics, he decided to become professional and join the French team Renault instead of competing for his country.

The renowned French cyclist Bernard Hinault was LeMond's mentor while he was racing for the Renault team and, subsequently, La Vie Claire. Hinault helped LeMond develop the tactics and mental fortitude that would be essential for success at the top levels of the sport. After competing in and placing third in his first Tour de France in 1983,

LeMond went on to win his first world title a few months later. While helping his master, Bernard Hinault, win a record-breaking fifth Tour de France in 1984, LeMond finished in second place. When LeMond won the Tour de France the following year, he did it by defeating Hinault.

A hunting mishap in 1987 almost killed LeMond when he was shot. Despite the fact that his organs were evacuated by emergency surgery, there were still two buckshot pellets in his heart lining and perhaps thirty in his legs and back. He got back on track for the 1989 Tour de France after an unsuccessful return in 1988. Just fifty seconds separated LeMond and Frenchman Laurent Fignon on the last day of the three-week competition, just before a 24.5-km (15-mile) time trial. LeMond won the Tour with the lowest margin of victory in the event's history, finishing 58 seconds ahead of Fignon. He defended his championship the year after that.

As a top performer in time trials and climbs, LeMond was a remarkable all-around rider. In 1985, he signed the first million-dollar deal, which elevated the overall wage level in the sport, and he was also a pioneer in technical improvements, including aerodynamic handlebars and helmets.

After being diagnosed with mitochondrial myopathy, a rare cellular condition that diminished his stamina, LeMond decided to withdraw from professional cycling in 1994. He went on to launch many bike-related businesses, the most notable of which was LeMond Fitness, an indoor exercise bike maker, in 2002. Lance Armstrong and Floyd Landis, two riders who later confessed to doping, were both first questioned by LeMond, a vocal opponent of PEDs. Despite a threat to publicly divulge LeMond's childhood sexual assault, he testified against Landis at his arbitration hearing in 2007, even though the caller had been identified as Landis's manager. Following his revelation of the threats during the hearing, LeMond joined the founding board of 1in6, a charity that assists male survivors of sexual abuse in childhood, later that year.

39

GEORGE BEST (SOCCER)

George Best was an Irish-born football (soccer) player who was one of the most prominent forwards in the history of the game and a stylish playboy off the pitch. He was born on May 22, 1946, in Belfast, Northern Ireland, and passed away on November 25, 2005, in London, England. It was in London that Best passed away. In the 1960s, the fashionable Best became one of the most recognizable characters associated with the "Swinging London" movement.

Best was sent to Manchester United by a local football scout from Belfast, who referred to the child as a "genius." Best was still a schoolboy when the recommendation was made. Best joined the club when he was 15 years old, and he made his debut by competing in the first division two years later, in 1963. During his second season with United, he scored goals that were difficult to score and helped the team win the league championship. He became an instant phenomenon. During the 1966–1967 season, he is credited with leading the team to yet another league title. United became the first English club to win the European Cup in 1968, and he was awarded the title of European

Footballer of the Year for his contributions to the team's success. Best scored a total of 178 goals throughout his tenure at United, which spanned 466 games.

The gorgeous Best, who was referred to as the "Fifth Beatle," had long hair, which was unusual among football players but was evocative of the "mop tops" worn by the Beatles, who were the most influential rock and rollers in England at the time. As was the case with them, Best was a massive celebrity. Additionally, his reputation extended beyond the realm of football; Best was the first of many players to become a frequent focus of the British tabloids. However, this fame also contributed to the development of a drinking problem that would ultimately prove to be his ruin. After leaving United in 1974, he went on to play for a number of smaller clubs in the United States, Spain, Australia, and Britain until 1983. His departure from United was a sad one. His drinking, on the other hand, continued to have an impact on his performance, and he rose to prominence not just for his evident brilliance but also for the potential that he had wasted. In 2002, Best got a liver transplant; nevertheless, he eventually was unable to overcome his alcoholism. He passed away as a result of a series of illnesses connected to the transplant that his damaged immune system was unable to fight off.

40

JIM BROWN (AMERICAN FOOTBALL)

Jim Brown was a legendary American football player who spent eight of his nine seasons atop the NFL's running charts. He was born on February 17, 1936, in St. Simons, Georgia, USA, and passed away on May 18, 2023, in Los Angeles, California. Many believe him to be the greatest running back of all time and the undisputed champion of his time. His acting career took off after that.

Brown was a spectacular athlete in every sport he played, from football to basketball to baseball to track and lacrosse, when he was a student at Syracuse University in New York. When Brown was a senior at Syracuse University, he was named to the All-America football and lacrosse teams. Both the Pro Football Hall of Fame and the U.S. Lacrosse National Hall of Fame inducted Brown, who was widely thought of as having excelled at lacrosse.

Brown was the NFL's leading rusher for the Cleveland Browns from 1957 to 1965, with the exception of 1962. A burly runner, Brown could outrun and even run over his opponents thanks to his height of 6.2

feet (1.88 meters) and weight of 232 pounds (105 kg). In seven of those years, he carried for over 1,000 yards. In 1958, with a 12-game schedule, he ran for 1,527 yards; in 1963, with a 14-game schedule, he ran for 1,863 yards; O.J. Simpson eclipsed that record in 1973. He ran for 237 yards in a single game on November 24, 1957, which was an NFL record; on November 19, 1961, he matched that mark. By the end of his career, he had set many records, including 126 touchdowns (106 on the ground), 12,312 yards gained (on an average of 5.22 yards per carry), and 14,811 yards gained (from both running and passing). The marks for both running and total yards were held by Brown until they were eclipsed in 1984 by Walter Payton of the Chicago Bears.

Brown left football for an acting career at the age of 30, when he seemed to be at the peak of his athletic ability. Among his many film credits are the blaxploitation features Slaughter (1972) and Three the Hard Way (1974), as well as the action and adventure features The Dirty Dozen (1967) and 100 Rifles (1969). Furthermore, he often appeared on television and was cast in comedies, including Mars Attacks! (1996) and She Hate Me (2004). Brown also formed organizations to aid Black-owned companies and rehabilitate gang members, demonstrating his active involvement in problems affecting African Americans.

Brown had many brushes with the authorities during his career, with numerous of them involving claims of domestic abuse. The verdict for the 1999 automobile vandalism case against his wife was guilty. In 2002, Brown spent almost four months behind bars instead of receiving probation that would have allowed him to comply with the court's conditions, which included counselling. Jim Brown: All American, Spike Lee's documentary, came out that year. Out of Bounds, an autobiography co-authored with Steve Delsohn came out in 1989.

41

ZINEDINE ZIDANE (SOCCER)

French soccer player Zinedine Zidane won the European Championship in 2000 and the World Cup in 1998. He was born on June 23, 1972, in Marseille, France. His managerial career took off after that.

Upon joining Cannes in 1989, Zidane immediately became the squad's offensive focal point, having previously played for the US Saint-Henri youth team. His towering stature and superb field vision matched his superb feet and upper-body power, making him an ideal midfielder. After being traded to Bordeaux in 1992, he had his best season with the club, scoring ten goals. Zidane made his international debut two years later and scored twice in 17 minutes against the Czech Republic. He was also awarded France's Best Young Footballer in that year.

While playing for Bordeaux in 1995, Zidane was instrumental in helping his team reach the UEFA Cup final. But he was sent to the Italian team Juventus the summer after that, and he quickly became just as beloved there as he had been in France. While playing for Juventus in

1997, Zidane was a part of the teams that won the Italian league, the UEFA Super Cup, and the World Club Championship. The 1997 and 1998 Champions League finals were also attended by Juventus. After Zidane signed with Real Madrid in 2001, the club won the European Super Cup and the Champions League that year. Zidane was voted FIFA World Player of the Year on three separate occasions (1998, 2000, and 2003).

Zidane had great success on a global stage as well. During the first 1998 World Cup in France, he had a thrilling experience. In the second round of the first round, Zidane was banned for two bouts for stomping on an opponent. Despite rumors that he might be benched, he made a triumphant comeback in the quarterfinals. Zidane scored twice as France defeated Brazil 3-0 in the World Cup final, claiming the trophy for France. France won the European Championship in 2000 under Zidane's leadership, and he was awarded tournament MVP.

France was a heavy favorite going into the 2006 World Cup despite the fact that it went scoreless in its 2002 championship defense. Zidane's spectacular play throughout the competition catapulted his squad to a championship match against Italy. Zidane was sent off for a red card after he head-butted an Italian player who had been teasing him towards the conclusion of second-half penalty time, with the score level at one and France having scored their only goal. Italy won the penalty shootout against France despite being without their captain. Zidane was named the tournament's best player and presented with the Golden Ball despite his humiliating elimination in the final. He hung up his cleats following the 2006 FIFA World Cup.

Zidane joined Real Madrid in 2013 as an assistant manager and, the following year was named manager of Real Madrid Castilla, the club's reserve squad in the top league. During a coaching change in the middle of the season in January 2016, he was elevated to the position of manager of Real Madrid. Zidane won the 2016–17 La Liga championship with Real Madrid. Also, during his leadership, the club won the Champions League in 2015–16, a feat they repeated in 2016–17 and 2017–18. He abruptly left his management role days after the 2018 Champions League final, saying he felt the club needed a new culture. But his break from coaching was short-lived; he returned to Real's helm in March 2019, immediately after the club's elimination from the Champions League. Another La Liga victory came the following year for Real Madrid.

42

DIEGO COSTA (SOCCER)

Botafogo striker Diego da Silva Costa plays in the Campeonato Brasileiro Série A.

After playing in Brazil, Costa joined Braga at 17 in 2006. He never played for the club but was loaned to Penafiel and joined Atlético Madrid the following year. His following two seasons were loaned to Braga, Celta Vigo, and Albacete. He joined neighboring La Liga team Real Valladolid in 2009 and was their top goalscorer before returning to Atlético Madrid. Costa failed to start for Atlético and spent more time on loan at Rayo Vallecano, where he was the club's top scorer.

Costa returned to Atlético in 2011 with more responsibility. He scored several goals and helped the squad win La Liga, Copa del Rey, and UEFA Super Cup. Costa joined Premier League team Chelsea in 2014 for €35 million (£32 million) after impressing many large clubs. Costa won a League Cup and two Premier League championships in London. After a falling out with Antonio Conte, Costa returned to Atlético Madrid in a club record €56 million deal in 2018, winning the Europa League and Super Cup.

Costa has Brazilian and Spanish citizenship. He played twice for Brazil in 2013 before proclaiming his intention to represent Spain after receiving Spanish citizenship in September. He debuted for Spain in March 2014 and has since received 24 appearances and scored 10 goals, representing them at the 2014 and 2018 FIFA World Cups.

Costa, known for his anger, has been chastised and disciplined for multiple fights.

José de Jesus and Josileide had Costa at Lagarto, Sergipe, Brazil. His father named him after Argentine footballer Diego Maradona despite the enmity between the two countries, while his older brother is called Jair after Brazilian star Jairzinho. Despite playing street football, Costa did not think he would become a professional as a youngster, owing to his isolated surroundings. He now runs an all-cost football school in his hometown. Costa likes Palmeiras.

Costa failed a tryout with local club Atlético Clube Lagartense. At 15, he left Sergipe and came to São Paulo to work at his uncle Jarminho's business. Although he never played, Jarminho had football contacts and suggested his nephew to Barcelona Esportivo Capela, a club from the south of the city that offered an alternative to drugs and gangs for slum youngsters. No football coaching experience before joining this squad. He became a professional with the club, earning £100/ month, and participated in the under-18 Taça de São Paulo despite a four-month penalty for slapping and disrespecting the referee. He was sent out in the tournament's opening game, but Jorge Mendes, a famous Portuguese agent, offered him a contract at Braga. Costa's father advised him to join the local Associação Desportiva São Caetano instead of sending him to Europe, but he insisted on taking the chance.

Jair, who played on Diego's side, was smaller and more technically proficient but less focused; the two were seldom deployed together to avoid disputes. He never played professionally but tried out for Salvatierra for three months.

43

NOVAK DJOKOVIC (TENNIS)

One of the all-time great men's tennis players, Novak Djokovic, was born on May 22, 1987, in Belgrade, Serbia, Yugoslavia (now in Serbia). He set a new male record with 24 Grand Slam singles titles, including a record-breaking 10 in the Australian Open.

Djokovic began playing tennis when he was four years old and swiftly rose through the junior divisions. As a 14-and-under player in Europe and a 16-and-under player on the Continent before going professional in 2003, he overcame the challenges of growing up in war-torn Serbia in the 1990s. At the tender age of eighteen, Djokovic made his way into the ATP top 100. It was in July 2006 that he claimed his first ATP title. He fell to Roger Federer in straight sets in the 2007 U.S. Open final after making it to the quarterfinals of the French Open and Wimbledon. In 2008, Djokovic kept up his impressive form and became the first Serbian man to win one of tennis's four most famous singles championships—the Australian Open—after winning his maiden Grand Slam competition. At the 2008 Beijing Olympics later that year, he won bronze.

From 2008 to 2010, Djokovic won only 10 ATP men's singles events and made it to the final of a single Grand Slam event (the 2010 U.S. Open). During that time, his growth essentially came to a standstill. When he captained Serbia to their first Davis Cup triumph in December 2010, his luck changed. His 43-match winning run began with his Davis Cup triumphs and continued with his second Australian Open championship in January 2011. This stretch is the third longest in the Open era (since 1968). After losing to Federer in the semifinals of the French Open, Djokovic's incredible run came to an end. However, his great performance propelled him to the top of the world rankings soon after his 2011 Wimbledon victory against Rafael Nadal. Djokovic went on to win his third Grand Slam of the year after beating Nadal in the final of the U.S. Open.

After a five-set drama that lasted over six hours, he defeated Nadal once again at the 2012 Australian Open. In 2012, at the French Open, they met in the final for the fourth year in a row; Djokovic was defeated by Nadal in four sets. Djokovic won his fourth Australian Open title in 2013 by defeating Andy Murray, and he won Wimbledon again the following year by defeating Federer in a thrilling five-set final. Djokovic became the all-time leading men's singles winner at the Australian Open during the Open era in 2015 when he defeated Murray to win his fifth career title. Federer lost against top-ranked Djokovic in the 2015 French Open final, but Djokovic bounced back to win Wimbledon for the third time. He won his tenth Grand Slam championship in the U.S. Open, continuing his hot streak, by defeating Federer in the final. In the 2016 Australian Open final, Djokovic extended his winning run in Grand Slam events to 21 matches with a straight-set victory against Murray. Once again, he defeated Murray in a Grand Slam final in 2016 at the French Open. Djokovic completed his career Grand Slam with his first French Open title.

But in 2023, Djokovic went back to Australia, which had loosened its COVID-19 regulations. He equaled Nadal for the Grandest Slam men's singles titles that year with his tenth triumph at the Australian Open. After winning the French Open a few months later, Djokovic asserted his ownership of the record. He reached Wimbledon's finals in 2023 before losing in a thrilling five-set match against Carlos Alcaraz. With a triumph at the U.S. Open, Djokovic bounced back and won his 24th Grand Slam tournament.

44

MARTA VIEIRA DA SILVA (SOCCER)

Marta is a Brazilian athlete who was born on February 19, 1986, in Dois Riachos, Brazil. She is generally regarded as the best female soccer player that has ever lived. Three times between 2006 and 2010, and again in 2018, Marta was named FIFA World Player of the Year.

When Marta was a little girl, she practiced football on the streets of her little town using deflated footballs that she had been lying about and makeshift balls made of wadded-up grocery bags because she couldn't play with her male classmates. At the age of fourteen, she had already joined a local boys' junior squad and was playing for them when a scout from the renowned Rio de Janeiro men's football club Vasco da Gama, which was establishing a women's team, saw her. Afterwards, she participated in women's teams, first with Vasco (which disbanded a few years later), then with Santa Cruz in Brazil, and finally, in 2004, she joined Umeå IK in Sweden.

While playing for Umeå, Marta first became well-known for her role in the 2004 UEFA Women's Cup (now called the Women's Champions

League) and her contributions to the team's success in 2007 and 2008. In addition to helping Umeå win a Swedish Cup in 2007, Marta was instrumental in the team's four-year run of Damallsvenskan championships (the top level of women's domestic football in Sweden) from 2005 to 2008. During her five seasons with Umeå, Marta topped the league in goals for three consecutive seasons (2004, 2005, and 2008) and scored an incredible 111 goals in 103 league games. After signing with the WPS Los Angeles Sol in 2009, she departed from Europe. When her failing Los Angeles club dissolved in 2009, Marta was crowned WPS Most Valuable Player (MVP). She then relocated inside the WPS to join the Santa Clara, California team, FC Gold Pride. She won a WPS championship in 2010 while playing for the Gold Pride (and was named MVP for the league twice) and a second WPS trophy in 2011 with the Western New York Flash. Marta competed for Santos FC in her native country during the 2009 and 2010 WPS off seasons. Marta went back to Sweden and joined Tyresö FF when the WPS halted operations in 2012. In 2014, she transferred to FC Rosengård. After three years, she signed up with the Orlando Pride of the National Women's Soccer League in the US.

Thanks mostly to her achievements with the Brazilian women's national team, Marta cemented her position as the finest female player of her time. She debuted for Brazil's national team in the 2002 FIFA Women's World Cup when she was only 20 years old. After making the jump to the senior national team the next year, she helped Brazil reach the quarterfinals of the 2003 FIFA Women's World Cup with three goals. With seven goals at the 2007 Women's World Cup, she not only helped Brazil finish in second place, but she also earned the tournament's Golden Boot award. The Brazilian national team was once again defeated in the quarterfinals of the Cup in 2011, despite Marta tying Birgit Prinz of Germany for most Women's World Cup goals with fourteen throughout her career. The identical scoring scenario and opponent as her first World Cup goal occurred in 2015 when she scored her 15th Cup goal on a penalty kick against South Korea, setting a new record for Women's World Cup scoring. Brazil was eliminated in round 16 of the 2019 Women's World Cup, but she became the all-time leading scorer at the tournament with 17 goals. Miroslav Klose of Germany had previously held the record.

Marta also had a key role in Brazil's silver medal finishes in the 2004 Summer Olympics in Athens and the 2008 Summer Olympics in Beijing. She made history in the 2020 Tokyo Games as the first football player to score in five straight Olympics; however, Brazil fell in the quarterfinals. The games were held in 2021 because of the COVID-19 epidemic.

45

JOE LOUIS (BOXING)

Joe Louis was an American boxer who held the title of world heavyweight champion from June 22, 1937, when he knocked out James J. Braddock in eight rounds in Chicago, until his short retirement on March 1, 1949. He was born on May 13, 1914, in Lafayette, Alabama, U.S., and died on April 12, 1981, in Las Vegas, Nevada. His reign was the longest in the history of any weight category. He scored 21 knockouts while successfully defending his championship 25 times, more than any other champion in any division. However, he was likely unable to defend it many more times due to his duty in the U.S. Army from 1942 to 1945. He had a reputation for being a cheap knockout puncher with pinpoint accuracy.

Sharecropper Louis's father was confined to a state mental institution when Louis was around two years old. Louis, along with his eight siblings and his mother's second marriage, relocated to Detroit, Michigan, where he began his amateur boxing career. Louis has fifty victories and four losses in fifty-four amateur bouts; he was the 175-pound champion of the United States Amateur Athletic Union in 1934 and the Golden Gloves champion as well. On July 4, 1934, he had his first professional fight. Within a year, he had knocked out Primo Carnera, the first of six heavyweight champions who had either previously or later been defeated by him. The others were Max Baer, Jack Sharkey, Braddock, the German champion Max Schmeling, and Jersey Joe Walcott. Schmeling handed Louis his first professional defeat in 1936. After defeating Braddock and winning the championship in 1938, Louis faced Schmeling in a rematch that the American media depicted as a clash between democracy and Nazism, even though Schmeling was not a Nazi. Suddenly, a national hero, Louis, won by first-round knockout. He may have been the first Black American to gain widespread white admiration for his exceptional boxing abilities, but his sportsmanlike conduct in the ring (he refrained from gloating over his white opponents), his seemingly modest and mild-mannered personality, and his discretion in his personal life also contributed to this.

Money troubles persisted after Louis's second retirement, and he was compelled to work as a professional wrestler for a while. He then worked his way up to the position of greeter at Caesar's Palace, a casino and resort in Sin City, Nevada. Schmeling was a pallbearer during his funeral in 1981 when he was laid to rest in Arlington National Cemetery. Even after he passed away, Louis continued to be a symbol of Detroit. From 1979 to 2017, the Detroit Red Wings played their NHL games at Joe Louis Arena, and in 1986, a famous public monument honoring Louis was built in downtown Detroit. The monument features an arm with a clenched fist suspended in a pyramidal frame, measuring 24 feet [7.3 meters]. The International Boxing Hall of Fame admitted Louis in 1990, and the Ring Magazine Boxing Hall of Fame in 1954. The Congressional Gold Medal was bestowed on him after his death in 1982.

46

MERYL DAVIS AND CHARLIE WHITE (FIGURE SKATING)

Former ice dancers Meryl Davis and Charlie White are Americans. The couple is the 2014 Olympic Champion, 2010 Olympic silver medalist, two-time World champion (2011, 2013), five-time Grand Prix Final winner (2009–2013), three-time Four Continents champion (2009, 2011, 2013), and six-time U.S. national champion. They also won a 2014 Winter Olympics team bronze.

White and Davis partnered in 1997. They are the longest-running U.S. dance team. They are the first American ice dancers to win the World and Olympic titles. They were the first ice dance team to obtain level fours on all aspects at the 2006 NHK Trophy.

Davis started winter skating on a nearby lake at age five. She started ice dancing at age eight after skating alone. She reached Midwestern sectionals in novice women before abandoning singles for ice skating.

White started skating at 5. He earned the 2004 U.S. Novice Championships bronze medal in singles skating and skated internationally as a junior. He gave up singles skating after 2005–06 to concentrate on ice dance. White started ice dancing at seven on his coach's recommendation to improve his skating.

Davis's coach, Seth Chafetz, paired Davis with White in 1997. Davis noted in 2009: "Charlie and I grew up 10 minutes apart. Our parents are besties. We know each other well and have matured."

Davis/White earned the Juvenile Junior Olympics silver medal in their first season together. They won intermediate Junior Olympics gold in 1999–00.[4] They placed 6th as Novices in the 2001 U.S. Championships in 2000–01. They won silver as novices in 2001–02 and became juniors. In their junior debut, they finished 7th at the 2003 U.S. Championships after failing to medal at either Junior Grand Prix in 2002–03.

Davis/White won the 2003–2004 regional title and National junior silver medal. This got them to the 2004 Junior Worlds, where they placed 13th.

Davis/White won two ISU Junior Grand Prix bronze medals in 2004–2005. White fractured his ankle before Sectionals, preventing Davis/White from qualifying for the 2005 U.S. Championships. Their season finished.

Davis/White won two Junior Grand Prix tournaments and came second in the Final in 2005–2006. They won the 2006 U.S. Championships junior national championship and the 2006 Junior Worlds bronze medal. Davis left Juniors after that season. After White fractured his ankle during a 2006 hockey tournament, they missed training time.

47

LARRY HOLMES (BOXING)

Larry Holmes was an American heavyweight boxing champion who was successful in the late 1970s and early 1980s. He was noted for his strong defense and was born on November 3, 1949, in Cuthbert, Georgia, in the United States.

At a youth facility in Easton, Pennsylvania, Holmes, who had been a street fighter in his younger years, attempted to enter the world of organized boxing. Before going professional at the age of 24, he had already won 19 of his 22 bouts and various championships prior to that. During the middle of the 1970s, he served as a sparring partner for both Muhammad Ali and Joe Frazier, who were both contending for the title of heavyweight champion. As a result of the presence of these two great heavyweights in competition, Holmes had a tough time establishing himself as a fighter of the highest caliber and found it challenging to get into top-level contests.

Between the years 1973 and 1978, Holmes won a total of 28 straight fights, culminating in a victory against the defending champion Ken Norton on June 9, 1978, which resulted in a 15-round decision.

This victory claimed the heavyweight title from the World Boxing Council (WBC). From 1978 to 1983, Holmes successfully defended his championship seventeen times, beating great fighters like Earnie Shavers, Leon Spinks, and Gerry Cooney during the course of his career. On October 2, 1980, Holmes competed against the renowned Ali, who was in the process of making a return at the age of 38. After eleven rounds, Holmes was able to establish his position as the heavyweight champion of the world. However, Holmes had a great deal of emotional distress throughout the battle. He considered Ali to be a close friend, and since this bout took place after Ali had reached his peak, Holmes found himself in the situation of having to defeat, or more accurately, pummeled, his mentor.

Holmes gave up his World Boxing Council championship in 1983, but his conflicts with boxing promoter Don King continued throughout the year. Despite this, the International Boxing Federation continued to recognize him as the heavyweight champion. He successfully defended his title three times until ultimately losing it to Michael Spinks in a decision that was decided after fifteen rounds on September 21, 1985. Following the defeat, which was Holmes's first in 49 fights, he decided to retire, which prevented him from tying Rocky Marciano's career record of 49 wins and 0 losses.

After coming out of retirement in 1986, Holmes was defeated by Michael Spinks in a rematch to end his career. Holmes made his comeback to the ring once again in 1988, this time to face heavyweight champion Mike Tyson. The fight was stopped by the referee in the fourth round after Holmes had already been knocked down three times in the first three rounds. Holmes prevailed over his opponent Ray Mercer in 1992, which allowed him to progress to the championship fight against Evander Holyfield, who ultimately prevailed over him by decision. Holmes attempted to fight Oliver McCall for the WBC heavyweight championship on April 8, 1995, but he was unsuccessful and lost in 12 rounds. On January 24, 1997, Holmes faced Brian Nielsen for the heavyweight championship of the International Boxing Organization (IBO). However, he was unsuccessful in his attempt to capture the belt. Holmes had previously won his previous four contests. At the time of his retirement in 2002, Holmes had a record of 69 victories (44 of which were achieved by knockout) and six defeats. In the year 2008, he was honored with induction into the International Boxing Hall of Fame.

48

DAN GABLE (WRESTLING)

Dan Gable is an American freestyle wrestler and coach who was born on October 25, 1948, in Waterloo, Iowa, United States. He is consistently regarded as the most accomplished amateur wrestler in the history of the United States.

Gable went through high school competition without suffering a single loss and went on to win three straight Iowa state high school titles. He had a record that was very close to flawless when he was competing for Iowa State University. While he was still a freshman, he competed in the Midlands Tournament, which is a major wrestling tournament in the United States. He won the first of his six wins in that competition, which included victory against two national champions. Both in 1968 and 1969, Gable was victorious in the National Collegiate Athletic Association (NCAA) championship game. Additionally, he established a new record for the most straight collegiate wins with 100. throughout his final year at Iowa State, Gable was defeated by Larry Owings, a sophomore from the University of Washington, in the NCAA 142-pound national championship match. This was the only match that Gable was ever defeated in throughout his amateur wrestling career. Following his graduation, Gable participated in a rigorous training programme and went on to win both the world championship and the Pan-American title in 1971. Gable did not lose a single point throughout his six bouts in the Olympic Games held in Munich in 1972. As a result, he became the first American to win a wrestling gold medal in the last twelve years.

1972 marked the beginning of Gable's career as a wrestling coach at the University of Iowa, where he served as head coach from 1977 to 1997. It was under his direction that the Iowa squad achieved exceptional levels of success, as seen by their 15 NCAA championships and 21 Big Ten championships. The United States Olympic teams in 1980, 1984, and 2000 were all coached by him, and he also served as an assistant coach in 1988. In 1980, Gable was inducted into the United States Wrestling Hall of Fame, and in 1985, he was inducted into the United States Olympic Hall of Fame. The Presidential Medal of Freedom was bestowed on him during the year 2020.

49

CHRIS EVERT (TENNIS)

Chris Evert was an accomplished American tennis player who flourished in the sport throughout the middle and late 1970s and continued to be a key contender until the late 1980s. Evert was born on December 21, 1954, in Fort Lauderdale, Florida, in the United States. In addition to being known for her consistency, accuracy, composure, and grace, she is often credited with popularizing the two-handed backhand stroke.

Early on in her life, Evert, who is the daughter of a well-known tennis player, started receiving tennis instruction from her father. The quick evolution of her technique resulted in the development of a strong two-handed backhand and a level of focus that often-caused opponents to become uneasy. She defeated Margaret Smith Court, who was rated number one, when she was just 15 years old, and in 1971, she became the youngest player to go to the quarterfinals of the United States championship. Her first Wimbledon competition was the following year when she won the Virginia Slims tournament. She also made it to the semifinal round in her maiden Wimbledon tournament.

Beginning in December 1972, Evert began her career as a professional. In March 1973, she triumphed in her first professional event, and shortly thereafter, she graduated from high school. The incredible 56-match winning run was capped by victories at Wimbledon, the French and Italian championships in 1974, and the French championship in 1974. Especially when both players won the singles titles at Wimbledon in 1974, the media paid significant attention to her connection with tennis legend Jimmy Connors, which eventually led to her engagement to him. However, the pair ultimately decided to break off their engagement. In 1975, she was able to keep both her Italian and French crowns, and in the same year, she also won the first of four consecutive U.S. Open titles (1975–78), making her the first woman to do so since Helen Hull Jacobs. This was her second Wimbledon championship, which she won in 1976. She possessed one of the most remarkable records in tennis when it came to clay-court play; as of April 1978, she had not lost a single match on clay in 118 matches over 24 events. This was despite the fact that she had experienced some difficulties on grass courts on occasion.

After being married to tennis star John Lloyd in 1979, she changed her name to Evert Lloyd. The pair split in 1987, and Evert Lloyd became her new identity. The United States Open (1980 and 1982), Wimbledon (1981), the Virginia Slims (1987), the French Open (1979, 1980, 1983, 1985, and 1986), and the Australian Open (1982 and 1984) were among the tournaments in which she won, adding to her already impressive list of accomplishments.

The year 1989 marked her retirement from the professional tennis circuit, after which she went on to become a television commentator, a special consultant to the United States National Tennis Team, and the president of the Women's Tennis Association from 1982 to 1991. Chris Evert Charities, which largely addresses issues related to substance abuse and family dynamics, was also established by her. She co-founded the Evert Tennis Academy in Boca Raton, Florida, in 1996 in collaboration with her family. Evert tied the knot with Greg Norman, an Australian golfer, in 2008; however, the couple divorced the following December.

Evert has been honored with a number of accolades, including being selected as the Female Athlete of the Year by the Associated Press on four separate times. Additionally, in 1985, the Women's Sports

Foundation recognized her as the most accomplished female athlete in the preceding quarter of a century. 1995 was the year that she was admitted into the International Tennis Hall of Fame, and the decision was unanimous.

50

CHRIS FROOME (CYCLING)

Cyclist Chris Froome was born on May 20, 1985, in Nairobi, Kenya. He won the Tour de France four times: in 2013, 2015, 2016, and 2017.

After Froome's father's bankruptcy, his British parents split, and he was born in Nairobi. After his mother supported his passion for riding, the family relocated to South Africa. There, he received an education and, at the age of 12, started training with David Kinjah, a Kenyan cyclist. Kinjah accompanied Froome on bike rides in the dusty rural hills close to Nairobi with elderly local Kenyan riders. Froome picked up some Swahili and a little of Kikuyu, a regional language. He went to boarding school in South Africa and then spent two years at the University of Johannesburg studying economics; nevertheless, he chose to become a cyclist instead of an accountant, unlike his two brothers.

After becoming a professional in 2007, Froome competed for the South African team Konica Minolta when she was 22 years old. He rode in the 2008 Tour de France with the South African-sponsored team Barloworld and finished in eighty-fourth place. British instructor

Rod Ellingworth saw him and was so taken by his climbing abilities that he was prepared to overlook his lack of expertise and propensity to fall on the twisting Alpine descents. Ellingworth suggested that Froome get a British racing licence so he could learn from the British teams' expertise, even though he competed for Kenya. Froome carried a British passport. Although he was afflicted with the parasitic ailment schistosomiasis for a significant portion of that year, he joined Team Sky in 2010. He placed second in the Vuelta a España (Tour of Spain) the year after, and in 2012, he finished second in the Tour de France behind Bradley Wiggins, who won for British Team Sky.

In 2013, while also being named the year's best rider by the Velo d'Or, Froome won the Tour de France for the first time. In the same year, he was also named Team Sky captain. In 2015, he repeated as Tour de France winner. There were rumblings that he may have taken PEDs due to his very high level of performance. Following the 2015 Tour, Froome made public the findings of his physiological testing in an attempt to dispel such rumors. Despite suffering two crashes, having to sprint uphill on foot due to bike damage, and executing a daring downhill attack while lying prone on his handlebars in an aero position, Froome became the first Tour de France winner in over twenty years to successfully defend his title the following year.

Froome suffered many injuries, including a fractured hip, after a catastrophic incident in June 2019 at the Critérium du Dauphiné in France. It wasn't until the UAE Tour in February 2020 that he got back into racing. Unfortunately, the coronavirus epidemic forced the cancellation of the event in the middle of the race.

51

MARK SPITZ (SWIMMING)

During the 1972 Summer Olympics held in Munich, the American swimmer Mark Spitz made history by being the first athlete to win seven gold medals in a single competition. Spitz was born on February 10, 1950, in Modesto, California, in the United States.

Spitz, along with a great number of other exceptional swimmers from the United States, had his training at the Santa Clara (California) Swim Club for a number of years. During his time at Indiana University, Bloomington, where he graduated in 1972, he successfully led the intercollegiate swimming team as captain. It was during the 1968 Olympic Games in Mexico City that he made a public prediction that he would win six gold medals. This prediction caused a lot of controversy. In point of fact, he only managed to win two, and both of them were team relay competitions, namely four x 100-meter and four × 200-meter freestyle events. Two individual medals were awarded to him: a silver medal for the 100-meter butterfly and a bronze medal for the 100-meter freestyle.

Spitz was outstanding at the Olympic Games held in Munich in 1972. He won all four individual men's competitions that he competed in, including the 100-meter and 200-meter freestyle races (with a time of 51.2 seconds and 1 minute and 52.8 seconds, respectively), as well as the butterfly race over the same lengths (for a time of 54.3 seconds and 2 minutes and 0.7 seconds). As a part of the United States men's swimming team that won three more gold medals but also established world records in the 400-meter medley relay, the 800-meter freestyle relay, and the 400-meter freestyle relay, he added three more gold medals to his collection. He held the record for the most gold medals won at a single Olympic competition until 2008 when it was surpassed by Michael Phelps, an American swimmer. In 1983, Spitz was also a member of the first group of athletes to be inducted into the United States Olympic Hall of Fame. In 1992, he made a temporary departure from retirement in order to compete in the 50-meter butterfly event at the Olympic Games. However, his effort to qualify for the squad was unsuccessful.

52

BONNIE BLAIR (SPEED SKATING)

An American speed skater named Bonnie Blair was one of the most successful athletes in the sport. Blair was born on March 18, 1964, in Cornwall, New York, in the United States. She won five gold medals and one bronze medal in the sprint events at three different Olympic Games (1988, 1992, and 1994), and she was the dominant athlete in all of them.

As a member of a family that has a strong passion for skating, Blair started competing in races when she was only four years old. The first time she was recognized for her accomplishments was in 1986 when she won the world short-track championship in Chamonix, France. In the next year, she achieved two world records in the 500-meter race on the standard circuit at the same time. She was victorious in her maiden global sprint title in 1989. 1994 was the year that she won the global sprint championship once again, in addition to winning the 500-meter and 1,000-meter events at the global Cup that same year. Moreover, she won these championships in 1995.

Despite the fact that she began poorly, Blair's biggest success came during her time in the Olympics. It was only possible for her to finish eighth in the 500-meter race in the 1984 Games held in Sarajevo, which was then located in Yugoslavia and is now located in Bosnia and Herzegovina. She was a favorite in the sprint events at the 1988 Games, which were held in Calgary, Alberta, Canada. She won the gold medal in the 500-meter event and the bronze medal in the 1,000-meter event by competing in the sprint events. Not only did she win the gold medal in the 500-meter and 1,000-meter races in the 1992 Olympic Games held in Albertville, France, but she also won the gold medal in both of those categories at the 1994 Olympic Games held in Lillehammer, Norway.

Blair had a technique that was almost perfect despite the fact that she was rather short for a speed skater. She was able to maintain an emphasized crouch and a smooth rhythm in her strides for the whole of the race, while other skaters generally lost time due to minor failures in their technique. She was an extraordinarily consistent skater.

53

SONNY LISTON (BOXING)

Sonny Liston (born May 8, 1932, St. Francis County, Arkansas, U.S.—died December 30, 1970, Las Vegas, Nevada) was an American boxer who was world heavyweight boxing champion from September 25, 1962, when he knocked out Floyd Patterson in the first round in Chicago, until February 25, 1964, when he stopped fighting Cassius Clay (afterwards Muhammad Ali) before the seventh round at Miami Beach, Florida.

While serving two lengthy sentences in jail, Liston, who was the son of a tenant farmer, is reported to have learned how to box during his time there. Despite the fact that he stated that he was born in 1932, there is evidence to suggest that he may have started his career in the ring as early as 1934 when he was 17 years old and using the name Charles ("Sailor") Liston. In the event that this is accurate, he was 45 years old at the time that he came out on top.

Both Liston's hitting strength and his longevity earned him a lot of respect. Beginning with his first fight, which was documented in

1953, and continuing until 1970, Liston, who stood 6 feet 1 inch (1.85 meters) tall and weighed 215 pounds (97.5 kg), competed in 54 fights, winning 39 of them by knockout and losing only four of them. The only time he successfully defended his title was when he knocked out Patterson in the first round of their subsequent fight. However, in his subsequent fight, he complained of an injury after six rounds and refused to continue fighting Clay. The first round of Liston's rematch with Clay, which took place on May 25, 1965, resulted in his knockout death. It was discovered that he had passed away at his residence in Las Vegas, Nevada, on January 5, 1971. According to the information on his death certificate, he passed away on December 30, 1970.

54

FLORENCE GRIFFITH-JOYNER (TRACK AND FIELD)

Florence Griffith Joyner was an American sprinter who established world records in the 100-meter dash (10.49 seconds) and the 200-meter dash (21.34 seconds), which have been in place since 1988. Joyner was born on December 21, 1959, in Los Angeles, California, United States, and passed away on September 21, 1998, in Mission Viejo, California.

In an effort to improve her speed, Griffith began jogging when she was seven years old and chased jackrabbits. She enrolled at the University of California, Los Angeles, in 1980 and received her Bachelor of Arts degree in 1983. Her coach at the time was Bob Kersee. After winning a silver medal in the 200-meter event at the 1984 Olympics held in Los Angeles, she rapidly became a media sensation due to the fact that her fingernails were covered with stickers measuring 6 inches (15 cm) in length, and she wore eye-catching racing costumes. Despite this, she went into a semi-retirement state since she was dissatisfied with her performance. During the year 1987, she recommitted herself to the sport by being involved in a rigorous weight-training programme and making adjustments to her starting technique. It was in the same year that she tied the knot with Al Joyner, who had previously won the gold medal in the triple jump in 1984 and was the brother of Jackie Joyner-Kersee, who had won the heptathlon. The modifications brought about remarkable outcomes. After competing in the Olympic trials in 1988, Griffith Joyner established a new world record in the 100-meter sprint with a time of 10.49 seconds. This time was 0.27 seconds faster than the previous record, and it was more than half a second faster than her previous best. She won three gold medals in the Olympics held in Seoul later that year, including the 100-meter, 200-meter, and four-by-four-meter relay events. Additionally, she won a silver medal in the four-by-four-meter relay event. Griffith Joyner was honored with the Sullivan Award in 1988 for being the most outstanding amateur performer in the country. Drug testing indicated that she did not use any prohibited chemicals despite the fact that her outstanding achievements aroused accusations of steroid usage.

Following his retirement in 1989, Griffith Joyner formed a foundation for children from disadvantaged backgrounds. Additionally, he served as the co-chair of the President's Council on Physical Fitness from 1993 to 1995. In 1996, an effort to make a return was unsuccessful due to a leg injury. The year 1995 was the year when she was inducted into the Track and Field Hall of Fame.

55

BRUCE LEE (MARTIAL ARTS)

Bruce Lee, an American martial arts superstar who helped popularize the genre in the 1970s, was born on November 27, 1940, in San Francisco, California, United States, and died on July 20, 1973, in Hong Kong.

Although Lee spent his formative years in Hong Kong, he was born in San Francisco. His father's career as an opera singer and sometimes actor exposed him to the world of show business from a young age. When Lee Joon-ho made her film debut at an early age, she was cast as a street urchin or a juvenile offender. In order to protect himself, he joined local gangs and started training in kung fu when he was a youngster. Lee won the Hong Kong cha-cha championship in 1958 after taking dancing classes at the same time, which helped him improve his footwork and balance even more.

Lee's parents moved him to live in the U.S. soon after he turned 18 because they were becoming more and more worried about his street fights and interactions with the police. He resided with relatives in Seattle, Washington, where he attended the University of Washington to study philosophy and theatre after finishing high school. His first martial arts school was established in Seattle; in 1964, he moved to Oakland, California, to establish a second school. He started teaching jeet kune do, a style that he had invented around that time and which combined elements of old kung fu, fencing, boxing, and philosophy in place of more conventional martial arts. He was cast as the sidekick Kato in the 1966–1967 T.V. series The Green Hornet after catching the eye of a producer at a karate event in the Los Angeles region with a kung fu performance.

After The Green Hornet was cancelled, Lee struggled to find acting work and started teaching Hollywood luminaries, including Steve McQueen, jeet kune do privately to supplement his income. Lee shot to fame in 1969 for a sequence in the film Marlowe in which he karate- and kickboxed his way through a whole office. But he returned to Hong Kong in 1971, troubled by his failure to get additional acceptable parts. In 1971 with Tang Shan da Xiong (also known as Fists of Fury in the U.S. and The Big Boss in Hong Kong) and in 1972 with Jing Wu Men (also known as Fist of Fury in the U.S.U.S. and The Chinese Connection in Hong Kong), Lee starred in two films that shattered box office records across Asia.

Meng Ling Guo Jiang (1972; Return of the Dragon [U.S.], or The Way of the Dragon [Hong Kong English title]), Lee's third picture, was a combination of his interests in producing, directing, writing, and acting. He used his unexpected success at the box office to establish his own production business. After that, in 1973, Lee shot to popularity with the release of Enter the Dragon, the first collaboration between Hong Kong and American production firms. The picture was a smashing success all over the globe. His untimely demise occurred only six days before to the film's debut in Hong Kong. Officially, his cause of death was stated as oedema of the brain caused by an allergic reaction to a prescription for headaches, but admirers and historians continued to speculate about the unusual circumstances surrounding his demise. Game of Death, a film under production at the time, used stand-ins and cardboard cutouts of Lee's visage; it was released in 1978.

A huge cult following developed for Lee's films after his death. Many people believe that Lee changed the way Asians were portrayed in American cinema, and he certainly became one of the most famous figures in 20th-century pop culture. Dragon: The Bruce Lee Story, a biography with some fictionalization, was out in 1993. His son Brandon, who followed in his father's acting footsteps, tragically lost his life on the set of The Crow (1994) after being shot with a malfunctioning fake pistol.

56

ALAIN PROST (FORMULA 1)

Alain Prost was born on February 24, 1955, at Saint Chamond in the Loire, where his father Andre made kitchen furniture. Alain was a hyperactive youngster with unlimited energy that made up for his height. He was so passionate about wrestling, roller skating, and football that he fractured his prominent nose multiple times. He considered teaching gym or using his football skills as a job. Kart racing, found at 14 while on a family vacation in southern France, became his obsession. His hobby became an addiction, and he won multiple karting championships. He quit school in 1974 to race full-time, modifying engines and selling karts. Winning the 1975 French senior karting championship earned him a season in Formula Renault, where he won two championships before going to Formula Three. After winning the 1978 and 1979 French and European F3 championships, numerous Formula One teams wanted him. After significant consideration, he joined McLaren in 1980.

In his maiden Formula One season, he finished in the points four times but had multiple crashes, fracturing his wrist and sustaining a concussion. Alain had concerns about the McLaren team's management and mechanical difficulties that caused several of his accidents. He joined Renault after breaking his two-year deal amid animosity.

At the 1981 French Grand Prix in Dijon, a French driver won his first Formula One race. Alain remembers the moment that started his winning streak for the attitude adjustment it created. "Before, you thought you could do it," they stated. "Now you know you can." He won nine races in three seasons with Renault, but the winner became increasingly at odds with the home team's management, who blamed him for failing to win a championship, and with the French fans, who preferred his ragtag teammate Rene Arnoux, with whom Prost had a running feud. In 1984, Alain relocated his wife Anne-Marie and son Nicolas to Switzerland and raced again with McLaren, exhausted.

Alain Prost won 30 races, three championships, and two runners-up in six seasons with McLaren. He won the inaugural French World Championship in 1985. For the first time since Jack Brabham 26 years earlier, he won again in 1986. His 28th Grand Prix win in 1987 broke Jackie Stewart's 14-year record. Prost won seven of McLaren-Honda's 15 overall wins from 16 races in 1988. The excellent new teammate Ayrton Senna won eight races and the driving championship. Thus started the explosive rivalry that propelled two of the sport's top drivers to unparalleled success and scandal.

Alain Prost, known as 'The Professor' for his analytical racing style, required all his brainpower and driving skills to beat Senna. The Professor, like his idols Stewart and Lauda, kept up by beginning a race carefully, easing on the brakes and tyres, and then challenging late. The Brazilian's willingness to go all out (even in the wet, which Prost detested) put his French teammate behind in public appeal, resulting in Formula One's most acrimonious conflict.

McLaren ruled in 1989, and the Prost-Senna rivalry placed them in conflict. The Frenchman accused his Brazilian teammate of unsafe driving and getting too much attention from McLaren and Honda, turning mutual adoration into animosity. Their tumultuous season concluded in a contentious fight in the chicane at Suzuka when Prost intentionally shut off Senna and won his third driving championship before fleeing to Ferrari.

In his first year with Ferrari, Prost won five races and finished the 1990 season in Japan with only McLaren to beat him. Senna won his second driving championship after purposely hitting the Ferrari at Suzuka. "What he did was disgusting," Prost stated. "He is a man without value."

Ferrari fell behind in 1991, as Alain Prost lost a race for the first time in 10 years. His loud criticism of the Italian squad for losing the plan got him sacked before the season ended. He took a break from racing in 1992 to commentate on TV but returned in 1993 with Williams-Renault to win seven more races, taking his total to a then-record 51, and won his fourth driving championship. Considering having the despised Senna as his Williams teammate, The Professor retired, stating, "The sport has given me a lot, but I decided the game wasn't worth it anymore."

He hadn't completed the game. He returned to TV commentating and advised and tested for McLaren before purchasing Ligier in 1997 and renamed it Prost Grand Prix. The four-time winner, who folded in 2001, was embarrassed by the team's political and financial issues.

57

ZICO
(SOCCER)

Brazilian musician Zico was born into a lower-middle-class household in Rio de Janeiro on March 3, 1953. Zico was born in Portugal, and as the saying goes, "football is in the blood" of every Portuguese person. He often skips class to join the Juventude club, demonstrating his exceptional talents. They were a little-known Brazilian street squad, but once Zico joined, they shot to fame. There, he began his football career, and today, he manages some of the best clubs in the world as a professional coach.

Zico had the opportunity to play in a single game for the American soccer team in 1968 while he was still a member of Juventude. A reporter couldn't help but notice him because of his incredible goal-scoring abilities throughout the game. While Zico was a little boy, the reporter recommended that his father take him to the Flamingo, a legendary nightclub. In his younger years, he was a relatively weak player, but he gave 110% in every game. His time with Flamengo ended with a promotion to the senior squad after 116 matches.

Brasil, despite receiving substantial offers from other teams like AS Roma, Real Madrid, AC Milan, and many more, remained at Flamengo for twelve long years. Despite receiving offers from other top teams, he ultimately decided to sign with Udinese Calcio because of the over $10 million in compensation they offered. In only 697 games played for that team, he scored almost 400 goals, which is an incredible feat. His goal-scoring numbers are really phenomenal, yet he spent his whole career as an attacking midfielder. Despite his outstanding play for Udinese, he was only able to help the team win one championship during his two years there. His dynamic performance earned him the title of best player in the 1978 and 1982 World Cups.

Injuries he sustained at the 1982 World Cup forced him to depart from Udinese. After a four-year hiatus, he returned to Flamengo. When he declared his retirement from professional football in 1994, his final club was Kashima Athens Soccer Club.

Eventually, Zico would take over as manager of the Kashima Antlers, the club he played for till his last game. A new chapter in my life as a coach would begin then. Zico has coached for many teams, including Japan and Iraq, and national teams. His club management experience includes Kawasaki Antlers, CFZ, Fenerbahçe SK, Bunyodkor, CSKA Moscow, Olympiacos, Al-Gharafa, and FC Goa. The FC Goa of the Indian Super League is now under his tutelage.

58

MIA HAMM (SOCCER)

Mia Hamm is a female American football (soccer) player who became the first worldwide star in the women's game. She was born on March 17, 1972, in Selma, Alabama, as a member of the United States. She played forward for the United States national team, which won the World Cup title in 1991 and 1999, as well as the Olympic gold medal in 1996 and 2004. She was a key player for the squad. Her all-around talent, her fiercely competitive nature, and her natural ability to score goals earned her a great deal of respect. She left the national team in 2004 with 158 goals in international competition, which was the most goals scored by any player, male or female (her record was surpassed by countrywoman Abby Wambach in 2013). She retired from the varsity squad in 2004. FIFA, which stands for the Federation Internationale de Football Association, honored her with the Women's World Player of the Year award on two separate occasions (2001–2002).

The goal-scoring ability that Hamm displayed when he was a youngster attracted the attention of major collegiate programmes as well as the national team. At the age of 15, she became the youngest individual in the history of the United States to ever be selected for the squad. Hamm began her academic career at the University of North Carolina in Chapel Hill in 1989. By the time she graduated in 1994, she had been instrumental in the Tar Heels' achievement of four National Collegiate Athletic Association titles.

To date, Hamm has participated in 276 matches for the national team. In addition to winning the four major championships during her career, the United States women's national team also finished third in the World Cup tournaments in 1995 and 2003 and won a silver medal at the International Olympic Committee in 2000. They received an unusual amount of media attention for a women's sports team, particularly during the 1999 World Cup, which was hosted in the United States. Hamm was the star of the show. Her popularity, which persisted after her retirement, was comparable to that of the most well-known male sportsmen. Jerseys with her number 9 were very popular, and they were sold in large quantities.

In addition, Hamm was a professional soccer player between the years 2001 and 2003 for the Washington Freedom, a team that competed in the Women's United Soccer Association. She continued to be interested in the sport even after she retired from all competitive participation in 2004. It is noteworthy that Hamm became a co-owner of the Los Angeles Football Club of Major League Soccer in 2014. She joined her husband, the former baseball star Nomar Garciaparra, and a large number of other individuals in this endeavor. The club did not begin playing until 2018.

Aaron Heifetz and Hamm collaborated on the book "Go for the Goal: A Champion's Guide to Winning in Soccer and Life," which was published in 1999.

59

DEREK JETER (BASEBALL)

American professional baseball player Derek Jeter was born on June 26, 1974, in Pequannock, New Jersey, USA. He played shortstop for the MLB's New York Yankees and was widely considered a fan favorite. Jeter was named to many AL All-Star teams.

Jeter began his baseball career in Little League at the tender age of five while growing up in Michigan. He had a stellar high school baseball career, earning the Yankees' first-round selection in 1992 after posting an excellent record. His junior year hitting average was 557. He had a terrible debut with the Class A Tampa Yankees in the minor leagues, making 21 mistakes in 58 games. In 1993, Jeter was voted the South Atlantic League's Most Outstanding Major League Prospect, and in 1994, he was named Baseball America's Minor League Player of the Year, thanks to his steady improvement throughout the subsequent years.

As of 1996, Jeter started at shortstop for the New York Yankees. His rookie year was marked by a.314 batting average and 78 RBIs. The New York Yankees defeated the Atlanta Braves in the World Series, and he was voted American League Rookie of the Year. When the New

York Yankees beat the San Diego Padres in the 1998 World Series, it was their second straight championship. Batting a combined 375 in the Yankees' three playoff series in 1999, Jeter became known as one of the best postseason hitters in baseball, and the team repeated their 1999 World Series victory against the Braves. In 2000, when the New York Yankees became the first team since 1974 to win three straight World Series, Jeter was awarded Most Valuable Player (MVP) of the All-Star Game and the World Series. The Yankees beat the New York Mets.

As the finest shortstop in the American League from 2004–2006, Jeter earned the Gold Glove award three years in a row. In 2006, the same season he was nominated for the American League MVP, he doubled as the top overall hitter and best offence at a position, winning the Hank Aaron Award and the Silver Slugger Award, respectively. When Jeter hit 2,674 in his career in 2009, he broke the big-league record for most hits by a shortstop. The 2009 season came to a close with a World Series triumph for the New York Yankees against the Philadelphia Phillies. Jeter became one of just 28 players in MLB history to achieve the 3,000-hit milestone on July 9, 2011.

After a slump in 2010 and 2011, he bounced back in 2012 with a league-leading 216 hits and a 316-batting average. When he broke his ankle in the first game of the American League Championship Series (ALCS), his season was cut short. He didn't play in the rest of the Yankees' playoffs (which concluded in an ALCS defeat) and only played in 17 games of the 2013 season. After announcing his retirement before the 2014 season, Jeter retired in September of that year with 3,464 hits, good for sixth all-time in Major League Baseball.

In 2017, Jeter became the chief executive officer of the Miami Marlins after being a member of the ownership group that bought the team. All four of the Marlins' subsequent seasons ended in losses, with the exception of the 2020 season, which was cut short due to the pandemic. In that particular year, Miami made it all the way to the division series, only to be swept in three games. After resigning as CEO in 2022, Jeter also cut off all financial connections to the franchise.

60

BILLIE JEAN KING (TENNIS)

American tennis player Billie Jean King rose to prominence in the late 1960s because of her impact and game, which she began to develop in Long Beach, California, USA, on November 22, 1943. She competed in both singles and doubles during her career and won 39 major championships.

King had a natural talent for sports, even as a young boy. In 1961, she and Karen Hantz were the youngest pair to ever win the Wimbledon doubles tournament, which brought her to the notice of the worldwide community. After that, she won a record 20 Wimbledon titles (singles 1966–68, 1972–73, and 1975; women's doubles 1961–62, 1965, 1967–68, 1970–73, and 1979; mixed doubles 1967, 1971, and 1973–74), as well as titles in the United States (1967, 1971–72, and 1974), France (1972), and Australia (1968). Martina Navratilova tied her record at Wimbledon in 2003. With 27 major championships under her belt, she was perhaps the best doubles player of all time. She made history in 1967 by being the first woman since 1938 to win all three of the major tennis championships in the United States and Great Britain in the same year: singles, doubles, and mixed doubles.

After becoming professional in 1968, King broke the $100,000 win barrier in 1971, becoming the first female athlete to do so. In a highly publicized "Battle of the Sexes" match in 1973, she defeated an elderly Bobby Riggs. There has never been a tennis match with such a massive crowd and prize money before. She was a tireless advocate for female players' rights, instrumental in establishing a women's tour, and successful in securing sponsorship from businesses. She served as the Women's Tennis Association's first president (1974) and was a co-founder of the organization.

World Team Tennis (WTT) was formed in 1974 by King and her husband, Larry King (married 1965–1987). Being one of the first females to coach male professional players, King made history while serving as player-coach for the Philadelphia Freedoms. King resurrected the tournament in 1981 after the WTT went bankrupt in 1978. King came out about her gay romance that year, the same year her ex-secretary sued her for financial assistance. (The lawsuit was lost by her secretary.) King lost all of her endorsement deals after coming out as a lesbian, although she became the most famous female athlete to do so at the time. Following her split with Larry King, she came out as a lesbian and started fighting for equality for the LGBT community.

When King made history in 1984, she was the first female professional sports commissioner, working for the World Team Tennis League. That same year, she also resigned from playing tennis. Her three Hall of Fame inductions were in 1980, 1987, and 1990, respectively, at the Women's Sports Hall of Fame, the International Tennis Hall of Fame, and the National Women's Hall of Fame. In 2020, the Federation Cup was rechristened the Billie Jean King Cup in honor of the tennis great. King continued to play tennis and has coached several Olympic and Federation Cup teams since the mid-1990s. The National Tennis Centre, which hosts the U.S. Open, was renamed the Billie Jean King National Tennis Centre in August 2006 by the United States Tennis Association as a way to remember King. The President presented King with the Medal of Freedom in 2009. Collaborating with Kim Chapin in 1974, Frank Deford in 1982, and Johnette Howard and Maryanne Vollers in 2021, she released three autobiographies: Billie Jean, The Autobiography of Billie Jean King, and All In. Pressure Is a Privilege: Lessons I've Learned from Life and the Battle of the Sexes (2008), and We Have Come a Long Way: The Story of Women's Tennis (1988; with Cynthia Starr) were two of her previous works.

61

IVAN LENDL (TENNIS)

From 1985, when he defeated John McEnroe 7–6, 6–3, 6–4, until 1988, when he lost to Mats Wilander 6–4, 4–6, 6–3, 5–7, 6–4, Lendl was the No. 1 world-rated player for 157 weeks, three weeks off Jimmy Connors' record. Over 13 championship-filled years (1980-92), Lendl was the world's greatest for 270 weeks. The Adidas-clad Lendl was one of the two finalists in US Open men's singles title matches from 1982 to 1989. He reached 19 major singles finals (third most all-time), won eight, won 94 ATP championships in 144 chances, and won 49 non-ATP titles for 144 lifetime titles. His 1,071-243 (81.65%) record was impressive. His 1,314 matches played and 1,071 wins rank second behind Connors.

After Lendl defeated Czech Miloslav Mecir, 6–4, 6–2, 6–0, to win his second straight US Open on September 15, 1986, Sports Illustrated headlined its cover, "The Champ That Nobody Cares About," but Lendl might have been your first choice for a tennis team. He reached 47 major finals and semifinals. The number of ATP events Lendl attended, and his 334 career finals or semifinals are staggering.

The similarly stoic and unattached Björn Borg suggested Lendl as the next up-and-comer. Lendl was a tough opponent, but Borg won his fourth consecutive victory in five thrilling sets, 6–1, 4–6, 6–2, 3–6, 6–1.

The 175-pound, 6-foot-2 Father Jiri was a prominent Czechoslovakian tennis player, giving Lendl a solid tennis background. In 1978, Lendl won the French Open and Wimbledon boys' singles championships, making him the world's top junior player. Professionally, Lendl's strength and power made the difference. It took a relentless work ethic, hours of tennis and weightlifting. Despite his stature, Lendl never liked serve-and-volley, although he utilized it well when needed. He was a punishing baseliner with a powerful topspin forehand (tight and flat instead of high and looping) and one of tennis's most aggressive backcourt games. His health was impeccable. Lendl defeated Mats Wilander 6–7, 6–0, 7–6, 6–4 in the 1987 US Open final in 4 hours and 47 minutes. He seemed like he could have played another four hours. That afternoon, his dashing one-handed forehand, his main weapon, was effective against Wilander. He utilized it often and under duress to win the tournament. The running drives were often down the line or at extreme crosscourt angles for wins. Lendl's athletic shot-making garnered boisterous acclaim from Louis Armstrong Stadium's maximum audience. New York people love tennis.

Jimmy Connors said, "Nobody likes to see the ball coming back at you faster than you deliver it," after beating Lendl in the 1982 US Open final for the second year.

Lendl beat John McEnroe 3–6, 2–6, 6–4, 7–5, 7–5 at the 1984 French Open to win his first of eight major singles championships. After falling down 2-0 and 4-2 in the third set, Lendl rebounded. In 1986 and 1987, he defeated Mikael Pernfors 6–3, 6–2, 6–4, and Wilander 7–5, 6–2, 3–6, 7–6 at Roland Garros. He went 53-12 in Paris.

Lendl's eight straight US Open final appearances tied Bill Tilden's record (1918-25), although he won three fewer. Lendl defeated McEnroe in 1985 and Mecir 6-4, 6-2, 6-0 in 1986. He proved his tenacity by defeating Wilander 6-7, 6-0, 7-6, 6-4 in 1987. At Flushing Meadows, he went 73-13 in 86 games. Lendl won the 1989 and 1990 Australian Opens. Lendl won the 1990 championship because Edberg resigned in the third set after Mecir lost in straight sets (6–2, 6–2, 6–2). All-time in Melbourne: 48-10. Lendl reached the Wimbledon finals twice, losing to Boris Becker in straight sets in 1986 and Pat Cash in three sets in 1987. Though he never won a championship in 14 All England Club tries due to the grass's unsuitability for groundstrokes, his overall record was 48-14. He tied for seventh in major singles championships with eight.

One of the first tour players to frequently customize his racquet's string tension, balance, weight, and handle with Warren Bosworth, Lendl thought he had an advantage in racquet technology.

After a year of competing against the world's best, Lendl dominated the Tour Finals. He won the season-ending championship in 1981, 1982, 1985, 1986, and 1987, and the World Championship Tennis Finals in 1982 and 1985.

Lendl led Czechoslovakia to its lone Davis Cup Championship, 4-1 against Italy, in 1980 before a fanatical home crowd in Prague. He was faultless in seven singles and three doubles matches.

In his later years, Lendl had chronic back pain. They were so severe that he retired at age 34 after his 1994 US Open second-round defeat.

Lendl joined Andy Murray's coach on December 31, 2011, and helped him win his first two majors at the 2012 US Open and 2013 Wimbledon Championship, ending a 77-year drought for a British male tennis player. After two years, Lendl and Murray split in March 2014. The couple collaborated again in 2016–2017.

Lendl was one of TENNIS Magazine's 40 Greatest Players.

62

DOROTHY HAMILL (FIGURE SKATING)

Dorothy Hamill is a figure skater from the United States who was born on July 26, 1956, in Chicago, Illinois. She was the winner of the top prize in the women's figure skating competition at the 1976 Olympic Winter Games held in Innsbruck, Austria.

When Hamill was eight years old, he skated for the first time on a pond in his backyard. With the help of a private instructor, she was able to skate for up to seven hours every day by the time she was 14 years old. Carlo Fassi, a prominent figure in the world of skating coaching, was her instructor throughout the 1970s, and she lived and trained in Denver, Colorado. Hamill was able to achieve success as a result of his rigorous training, winning the global championship in 1976 and the United States national championship. She was the last female skater to win a gold medal in the Olympics (1976), and she did it without performing any triple leaps.

Not only is Hamill famous for her exquisite skating, but she is also famous for her hairstyle, which has been replicated by many people, and for her skate spin dance. She got her hair cut into a wedge shape a few years before the Olympics, which kept her hair short and out of her eyes. This was done just before the Olympics. A camel spin that is followed by a sit spin is what Hamill came up with when he devised the Hamill camel.

In 1977, Hamill started her career as a professional skater and began her career with the Ice Capades, which she would later eventually own and run (1993–1995). In addition to her performances with other skating organizations, she was included in a number of television special episodes. She achieved the World Professional Championships during the years 1983 and 1987. Both Dorothy Hamill's on and Off the Ice (1983), which Hamill co-wrote with Elva Clairmont, and A Skating Life (2007), which he co-wrote with Deborah Amelon, were written by Hamill.

63

HAILE GEBRSELASSIE (TRACK AND FIELD)

It is well known that Haile Gebreselassie is a champion in the long-distance running event. The year 1973 saw Haile being born in the province of Arsi in Ethiopia. He was one of nine siblings, and his family lived in a financially impoverished environment. Every morning, he was required to run ten kilometers to school, and then he had to run the same amount back home in the evening.

In spite of the fact that he suffered from asthma, he was so quick that his companions were never able to catch up to him. Soon after, his talent was recognized, and he was invited to participate in the selection process for the Ethiopian national athletics team. Therefore, the youngster was able to run faster than his trained colleagues despite not having received any official training.

After that, he went on to win two gold medals at the Olympic Games in the 10,000-meter race, and he also set a record by winning the Berlin Marathon four times. He was victorious in the Dubai Marathon for three consecutive years.

In addition to that, he was the global half champion in 2001 and won four world crowns in the indoor running competition. This idea for the Great Ethiopian Run was conceived by Haile Gebreselassie in the year 2001. He has broken 61 Ethiopian records and has established 27 global marks, spanning from the 1500-meter dash to the marathon. His accomplishments are really remarkable. After the year 2004, Haile shifted his attention to road racing and marathons. Despite the fact that he claimed, "I'm retiring from competitive running, not from running," he maintained his great career. He won a number of wins throughout the course of his career until ultimately retiring in 2015.

You are unable to stop running since this is my real life. For BBC Sport, he said. At one point in time, Haile was referred to by the media as "A man from another planet." It is still true that he holds the world record for the 20,000-meter dash, the one-hour race, and the 10-mile marathon. At the present moment, Haile holds the position of president of the Ethiopian Athletics Federation. He intends to join politics in order to help the nation's development. In addition, he serves as a mentor and spokesperson for the G4S 4 adolescent programme, which provides assistance to fourteen teenage athletes. In addition, he played himself in the film Endurance, which was released in 1999.

He is an illustrious individual who triumphed over a great deal of adversity in order to be the legend that he is today. Given that Haile has had such a remarkable career, it is not surprising that he has also achieved a great deal of success in the commercial sector.

64

WILMA RUDOLPH (TRACK AND FIELD)

Wilma Rudolph was an American sprinter who was the first American woman to win three track-and-field gold medals in a single Olympic competition. She was born on June 23, 1940, in St. Bethlehem, which is located near Clarksville, Tennessee, in the United States, and she passed away on November 12, 1994, in Brentwood, Tennessee.

When Rudolph was a youngster, she suffered from asthma and was unable to walk without the assistance of an orthopedic shoe until she was 11 years old. However, her dogged resolve to compete led to her being a standout athlete in the sports of basketball and sprinting when she was attending high school in Clarksville, Tennessee. Between 1957 and 1961, she was a student at Tennessee State University. In the year 1956, when she was sixteen years old, she participated in the Olympic Games held in Melbourne, Australia. She won a bronze medal in the 4 × 100-meter relay competition. She established a new world record for the 200-meter event in 1960, just before the Olympic Games that were held in Rome. Her time was 22.9 seconds. During the actual Games, she achieved a remarkable feat by achieving gold medals in the 100-meter sprint, where she tied the world record with a time of 11.3 seconds. Additionally, she won gold medals in the 200-meter dash and contributed to the 4 × 100-meter relay team, which achieved a world record of 44.4 seconds in a semifinal race. She was the champion of the 100-yard dash for the Amateur Athletic Union (AAU) from 1959 to 1962.

As a result of her exceptionally flowing technique, Rudolph became a fan favorite among both spectators and media. Her accomplishments as an amateur athlete earned her the Sullivan Award from the American Athletic Union in 1961. After she retired from running, Rudolph worked as an assistant director for a youth foundation in Chicago during the 1960s. Her primary responsibility was to establish girls' track-and-field teams. Subsequently, she championed the sport of running on a national level. She was inducted into the United States Olympic Hall of Fame in 1983, the International Sports Hall of Fame in 1980, and the National Track and Field Hall of Fame in 1974. She was a member of the first group of individuals to be inducted into these halls of fame. The year 1977 saw the publication of her autobiography, titled Wilma.

65

ALEX FERGUSON (SOCCER)

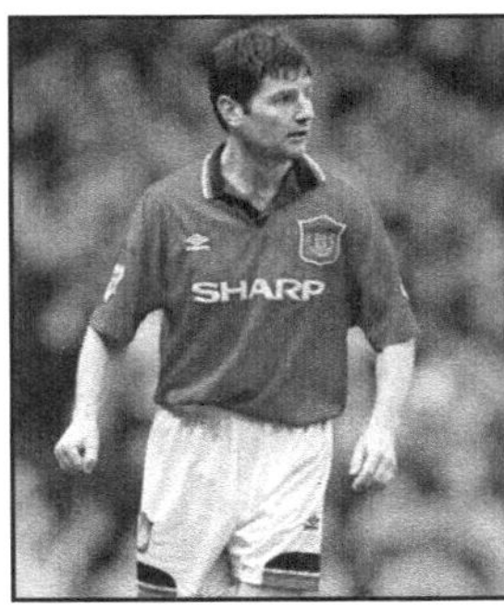

Scottish football (soccer) player and manager Alex Ferguson was born on December 31, 1941, in Glasgow, Scotland. He was most famous for his tenure as manager of Manchester United (1986–2013). With more than 30 domestic and international trophies under his belt, including 13 Premier League crowns, five Football Association (FA) Cups (1990, 1994, 1996, 1999, and 2004), and two Champions Leagues (1999 and 2008), Ferguson was the longest-tenured manager in "Man U" history.

While working as an amateur in a Glasgow shipyard, Ferguson joined the Scottish second-division football team Queen's Park when he was sixteen years old. In 1964, he joined Dunfermline Athletic of the First Division to begin his professional football career. Ferguson scored 31 goals in the 1965–66 Scottish League season, tying for the league lead. In 1967, his hometown Rangers paid a then-record £65,000 to get him. He retired in 1974 after two good but unremarkable seasons with the Rangers and two more teams.

After playing in his last game, Ferguson took over as manager of East Stirlingshire, a Scottish second-division club, in the summer of 1974. He joined St. Mirren a few months later and guided them to the 1976–77 league title. He took over as manager of Aberdeen FC in 1978. After three years in the Scottish Premier Division (1979–80, 1983–84, and 1984–85), four Scottish Cups (1982, 1983, 1984, and 1986), and a European Cup Winners' Cup (1983), Aberdeen had its most successful time under Ferguson's leadership. After receiving management offers from some of Europe's most famous teams in the years after his historic success with Aberdeen, Ferguson finally joined Manchester United in November 1986.

Manchester United's performance under Ferguson was erratic at first, with the club placing eleventh, second, eleventh, and thirteenth in the Football League's premier division during his first four seasons in charge. Until Manchester won the FA Cup to save the 1989–90 season, rumors circulated that he was on the brink of losing his job. With the win, United began their most successful managerial run in English football history, which would go on to win eight Premier League (the league's successor) championships and three FA Cups in eleven seasons, from 1992–1993 to 2002–03. At its peak, this era was capped off in 1998–99 by Manchester United's historic first "treble" (domestic top-division league, domestic cup, and continental championship) as the club not only won the league and FA Cup that year but also the Champions League. United won five Premier League championships in seven seasons, from 2006–07 to 2012–13, including a second Champions League in 2008, after a three-year league championship drought. After the 2012–13 Premier League season, Ferguson retired from playing football, although he remained with Manchester United in an administrative capacity and as an ambassador for the club.

On eleven separate times, Ferguson was recognized as the best manager in the Premier League. His autobiography was published in two volumes in 1999 and 2013. His many honors include a 1999 knighthood and a 1995 designation as Commander of the British Empire (CBE).

66

VALENTINO ROSSI (MOTOGP)

In February of 1979, born. An all-time great in the sport of racing, having won nine world championships. In 2004, I became a member of Yamaha, and I won four events on a Yamaha YZR-M1: in 2004, 2005, 2008, and 2009. Rossi is planning to leave Yamaha in 2011 in order to compete with Ducati in the MotoGP. Rossi moved up to the 500cc class beginning in the year 2000, after having previously won the GP125 championship in 1997 and the GP250 championship in 1999 on Aprilia machines. Beginning in 2001, he won the 500cc/MotoGP World Championships on Honda motorcycles for three consecutive years before retiring from the sport. He made the transition to Yamaha in 2004, and he didn't waste any time in winning the first round of the season. He went on to win the championship that year with a total of nine victories, including the triumph that he gained in the first round. With a total of eleven wins, he was able to reclaim the championship in the year 2005. During the years 2006 and 2007, he continued to compete for the championship title, but due to a string of unfortunate events, he ended up finishing in second and third place, respectively. In spite of this, he was able to reclaim the championship title in 2008 by accumulating a total of nine victories. With six victories, he once again won the championship in 2009. In a total of nine Grand Prix contests, Rossi was the champion and won the championship title eight times.

Despite the fact that he was forced to withdraw from four races due to injuries in 2010, he still managed to secure the third spot in the rankings. As he competed in the Malaysia Grand Prix of that year, he achieved his second victory of the season. It was his 46th victory on a YZR-M1, which was also his race number 46. Before approaching a turn, he would routinely push his inner leg out, which was a characteristic of his riding style that was characterized by tyre slides that were masterfully managed. In addition to that, he is widely regarded for his ability to set up and configure races efficiently. Additionally, he is well-known for his ability to amuse, and his many pranks are a source of joy for his followers. His motorcycle and helmet both have one-of-a-kind patterns on their surfaces.

67

ALLEN IVERSON (BASKETBALL)

American basketball player Allen Iverson was born on June 7, 1975, in Hampton, Virginia. He is famous for his spectacular on-court performance and his controversial off-court exploits. For the hip-hop culture, he was the first great athlete to have such a strong association.

Since he was a young athlete, Iverson has been the subject of both praise and criticism. The football and basketball teams he was a part of at Bethel High School won state titles during his junior year. His sentence was eventually overturned due to a lack of evidence, but he spent time in prison at the age of 17 after being accused of initiating a racially tinged altercation in a bowling alley. After accepting a scholarship to play college basketball at Georgetown University in Washington, D.C., he decided to depart after two years of averaging 23 points per game and winning the defensive player of the year honors from the Big East Conference. In the 1996 NBA Draft, the Philadelphia 76ers selected Iverson with the first overall pick.

Iverson won Rookie of the Year and led his club in scoring with an average of 23.5 points per game despite being one of the league's shortest players at 6 feet, 1.8 meters, and 165 pounds (75 kg). His trademark crossover dribble and lightning speed frequently rendered even the most skilled opponents defenseless. When he was off the court, he sported loose clothes, ostentatious jewelry, and braided hair—not exactly the image the NBA was going for. He had many brushes with the police during his first year in the league, was widely reported in the media as a selfish and disruptive player, and had regular confrontations with coaches and club officials. But he gained a legion of youthful admirers who related to his defiant persona.

Iverson established his skill on the court despite the issues that surrounded him. In 1998–99, he took the league scoring championship. In 2000–01, he led the 76ers to the NBA finals while capturing the scoring title, the steals title, and Most Valuable Player honors. He was moved to the Denver Nuggets in the midst of the 2006–07 season, when he was paired with rookie sensation Carmelo Anthony. Iverson became the sixth player in NBA history to achieve 20,000 career points in 2007, a testament to his exceptional scoring ability. But Denver didn't make it beyond the first round of the playoffs, and Iverson wanted to play for a team that could compete. After being moved to the Detroit Pistons three games into the 2008–09 season, Iverson and the franchise eventually parted ways due to the Pistons' dismal record and first-round playoff sweep.

After signing with the Memphis Grizzlies in September 2009, Iverson became dissatisfied with his position on the club and decided to leave after just three games. Shortly after, his contract was cancelled. Iverson signed with the 76ers in December 2009, but he returned for a second time after announcing his retirement from professional basketball. The 76ers had a temporary increase in home attendance with the return of the still-popular Iverson. The 76ers confirmed his departure from the club for the rest of the 2009–10 season the following month after he departed in February 2010 to be with his sick daughter. Iverson inked a two-year deal with the Turkish professional club Besiktas in October 2010. Until his formal retirement in October 2013, he remained without a club after leaving Besiktas in the middle of his debut season in Turkey. In 2016, Iverson was honored with his induction into the Naismith Memorial Basketball Hall of Fame.

68

ROBERTO DURAN (BOXING)

Roberto Durán was a Panamanian professional boxer who attained world championships in the weight classes of lightweight, welterweight, junior-middleweight, and middleweight. He was born on June 16, 1951 in Guararé, Panama.

During the beginning of his professional career, which started on March 8, 1967, Durán won the first 32 contests of his career, with 26 of those matches being won by knockout. However, on November 17, 1972, he suffered his first loss, which was a 10-round nontitle decision against Esteban De Jesús. In the earlier part of the same year, on June 26, Durán had defeated Ken Buchanan by knocking him out in the thirteenth round, claiming the title of world lightweight champion. Beginning in 1973 and continuing through 1978, Durán was victorious in each and every one of his following twelve contests for the lightweight title. This period of success lasted until 1978. Additionally, throughout this time period, he triumphed in every single one of his fights that did not include a championship.

After making the transition to the welterweight category, Durán obtained the world championship by virtue of a 15-round decision victory against Sugar Ray Leonard on June 20, 1980. However, in his subsequent bout, which took place on November 25, 1980, he was unsuccessful in retaining the title as Leonard knocked him out in the eighth round. Durán was not truly knocked out during the second encounter with Leonard after the first encounter. However, in a turn of events that became legendary, he refused to continue, and he surrendered in the middle of the round with the words "No mas!" (which translates to "No more!").

After resuming his career in the summer of 1981, Durán went on to win the junior-middleweight championship of the World Boxing Association in 1983 and the middleweight championship of the World Boxing Council in 1989. His formerly impressive victory record was slightly damaged as a result of his continued participation in boxing for such a long period of time (he was still fighting at the age of 49). He retired in 2002 with 103 wins and 16 defeats. In addition, his reputation was damaged as a result of the "No Mas" event with Leonard. On the other hand, boxing experts were in agreement that Durán was one of the best fighters of the 20th century when he was at the greatest point of his career. 2007 was the year that he was included in the International Boxing Hall of Fame list.

69

GARY KASPAROV (CHESS)

The 1985 world chess champion, Garry Kasparov, was born on April 13, 1963, in what is now Baku, Azerbaijan, U.S.S.R., but was originally from the Soviet Union. Kasparov became the first world chess champion to lose against a supercomputer in a competitive encounter and the youngest world chess champion at the age of 22.

Kasparov's father was Jewish, while his mother was Armenian. He started playing the game at the tender age of 6, became the Soviet youth champion at the tender age of 13, and won his first international event in 1979 at the tender age of 16. In 1980, Kasparov achieved the status of international grandmaster. He trained under Mikhail Botvinnik, a former world champion, from 1973 until 1978.

After surviving a series of elimination matches organized by the Fédération Internationale des Échecs (FIDE), the international chess organization, Kasparov faced up against reigning world champion

Anatoly Karpov in a showdown that took place in 1984–1985. Kasparov was on a four-game losing streak until he took a cautious defensive approach and went on an extremely lengthy streak of tied games against the champion. After 48 games, Kasparov had finally won three games against Karpov, but FIDE decided to end the series, a move that Kasparov strongly opposed. Kasparov became the youngest recognized champion in the game's history after a close victory against Karpov in a 24-game series in their 1985 rematch.

The Professional Chess Association (PCA) was founded in 1993 by Kasparov and English grandmaster Nigel Short, who both departed from FIDE. In retaliation, FIDE dethroned Kasparov as world champion; the same year, he won the PCA championship by defeating Short. He won his PCA championship again in 1995 after a successful defense against India's Viswanathan Anand; the PCA dissolved in 1996.

In a match that garnered attention all around the globe in 1996, Kasparov overcame Deep Blue, a sophisticated chess computer made by IBM. In 1997, Kasparov and the Deep Blue programming team decided to rematch. After having its intelligence enhanced, Deep Blue was able to emerge victorious. Kasparov conceded defeat to Deep Blue in the last game of the six-game competition after 19 moves. Russian Vladimir Kramnik defeated Kasparov in a championship match that lasted 16 games in 2000.

Although Kasparov did not stop being involved with chess in 2005, he did retire from competitive chess. Kasparov on My Great Predecessors was a critically lauded series of books he published between 2003 and 2006 that included biographies of every world chess champion, from Wilhelm Steinitz to Karpov and many more. Kasparov detailed his battle with Deep Blue in 1997 and praised technological advancement in his 2017 book Deep Thinking: Where Machine Intelligence Ends and Human Creativity Begins. Even after he retired from professional chess, Kasparov remained active, playing in exhibition matches and coaching other players.

In 2005, Kasparov chose to launch the United Civil Front, a political group opposed to Russian President Vladimir Putin, which kept him in the spotlight as well. In 2006, Kasparov was a major figure in the formation of the Other Russia, a loose confederation of political groups united in their desire to depose Putin. Although Other Russia failed to nominate Kasparov in time for the 2008 presidential election, he was chosen as their candidate in 2007 after many coalition-organized protest marches in which he and others were detained. He persisted in his criticism of Putin and released Winter Is Coming: Why Vladimir Putin and the Enemies of the Free World Must Be Stopped in 2015, continuing his outspokenness. Kasparov has been involved with The Wall Street Journal since 1991 when he was a contributing editor. By 2014, he has naturalized as a Croatian citizen.

70

ELINA SVITOLINA (TENNIS)

Ukrainian tennis star Elina Svitolina has become a big force on the women's circuit with her steady performance and effective groundstrokes.

Svitolina's quickness and battling skills have garnered recognition as the first Ukrainian woman to enter the WTA singles top 10. She should make significant Grand Slam gains and challenge the best players in the future.

Svitolina is versatile and can pivot between offence and defense. She plays largely from the baseline and exploits opponents' speed.

Svitolina is balanced off both sides and equally comfortable on her backhand and forehand. She seldom goes to the goal and prefers to play from behind.

Ukrainian forehands have topspin, whereas backhands are flatter. Movement and consistency are Svitolina's strengths. She is quick at the baseline and can catch more balls than other players.

She can lead rallies with her strong groundstrokes, particularly against lower-ranked competitors. Their Backhand, particularly down the line, is her strongest wing, although her forehand is also good.

Svitolina exploits her anticipation to dominate return games. She can rapidly position herself and neutralize most points since she can predict the serve's trajectory.

Ukrainians struggle to serve and are frequently pressured to hold. She has poor volleying technique, which makes her appear out of place at the net on rare occasions.

Born in Odesa, Ukraine, Svitolina is sporty. Father Mikhaylo Svitolin wrestled, and mother Olena Svitolina rowed professionally.

Andre Agassi was her tennis idol when she began playing at five. She started playing tennis to get her father's attention, but she fell in love with it.

When businessman Yuriy Sapronov saw Svitolina's skills and sponsored her training, her family relocated to Kharkiv in 2008. Since then, they have lived in Kharkiv, although Elina often visits her Monte Carlo home.

Her junior career was very successful, winning the 2010 French Open girls' championship. Eugenie Bouchard defeated her in the 2012 Wimbledon girls' final.

Svitolina is a regular at Grand Slams and the top of women's tennis. With so much time left, she should have a Hall of Fame career.

71

DANIIL MEDVEDEV (TENNIS)

At each and every level of the ATP event hierarchy, Medvedev has achieved the title of champion.

It is worth noting that all of his triumphs at the Masters have been achieved on hard courts, and his only Grand Slam victory to yet came at the 2021 US Open.

Since the beginning of his career, Medvedev has only competed in one clay court final, which he lost to Dominic Thiem in Barcelona in April of 2019.

Since Andy Roddick in February 2004, Medvedev became the first guy from outside the Big Four to hold the world No. 1 ranking. This accomplishment occurred about 18 years after Roddick's achievement in February 2022.

He is the third Russian player to reach the top of the ATP Rankings, following in the footsteps of Yevgeny Kafelniko and Marat Safin. He is also the 27th man worldwide to achieve this feat.

It has been shown that Medvedev has one of the greatest backhands on tour, and he is also known for his ability to counterpunch. He will often advocate giving himself time by staying as deep as he can in the court; nonetheless, it is arguable that this technique is the reason he has struggled on clay and grass courts.

In spite of the fact that he has had difficulties on clay courts, Medvedev is one of the most difficult players to defeat on hard courts. He has also shown improvement on grass courts, despite the fact that he was not allowed to compete at Wimbledon in 2022 due to the ban on players from Belarus and Russia.

In light of the fact that Daniil Medvedev's driving license in Monaco was revoked as a result of an incident involving speeding, he is experiencing a sense of urgency. He is the proud owner of a number of sports automobiles, and when he is not on Tour obligations, he enjoys taking them out for rides. His collection of automobiles is rather spectacular, and although he has a liking for BMWs, he also has a few Mercedes in his collection.

During the month of September 2018, Daniil Medvedev tied the knot with his longtime love, Darya. The pair just recently became parents for the first time, which coincided with the tremendous tennis baby boom that occurred in October of 2022. Medvedev has, for the most part, managed to keep his family out of the public eye and has only sometimes mentioned them on his various social media platforms. On the other hand, more often than not, you will see Daniil Medvedev in court on his official social networks.

Beginning in 2021 and continuing through 2022, Daniil Medvedev was the seventh-highest-paid tennis player. He is reported to have a net worth of twenty million dollars. The role of brand ambassador for BMW in Russia is now held by Medvedev.

There is a growing impression that his sponsorship portfolio is expanding despite the fact that certain firms are avoiding backing Russian sportsmen.

Since soon before the pandemic struck, Daniil Medvedev has been a player who has been performing at a consistently high level with his performance. His victory in the 2022 Australian Open came dangerously close to adding to his victory at the 2021 US Open; nevertheless, he was ultimately defeated by Rafael Nadal's incredible comeback. Also, Medvedev triumphed in the finals of the 2020 ATP Tour, indicating his entrance as a formidable opponent.

Tecnifibre is the company that provides all of Medvedev's rackets, while the world-famous Lacoste brand is the one that sponsors his gear.

The fact that he has a well-documented passion for gaming would be beneficial to him in terms of obtaining an endorsement from HyperX.

Moreover, he has received sponsorships from Bovet and Tinkoff, and in 2021, he made $8 million from these deals.

72

JACK NICKLAUS (GOLF)

Jack Nicklaus is a professional golfer from the United States who was a dominant figure in the world of golf from the 1960s to the 1980s. Nicklaus was born on January 21, 1940, in Columbus, Ohio, in the United States.

Nicklaus accomplished the feat of winning the United States Amateur Championship in both 1959 and 1961 when he was a student at Ohio State University. In the same year, 1961, Nicklaus established a new record for the highest score ever achieved by an amateur in the United States Open, which was 282. Jack Nicklaus's own comments on his career in the United States Open may be found in the book titled "U.S. Open: Jack Nicklaus in his own words." Jack Nicklaus won the Masters Tournament six times (1963, 1965, 1966, 1972, 1975, 1986), the U.S. Open four times (1962, 1967, 1972, 1980), the Professional Golfers' Association of America (PGA) Championship five times (1963, 1971, 1973, 1975, 1980), and the British Open

(Open Championship) three times (1966, 1970, 1978). All of these victories occurred after Nicklaus turned professional in 1962. Among his successes in other countries, he won six championships at the Australian Open. Nicklaus was a record three-time solo World Cup champion (1963, 1964, 1971), and he was a part of the United States team that won the World Cup six times (1963, 1964, 1966, 1967, 1971, 1973). As of the year 1986, he had participated in one hundred major championships and had made it to the top three 45 times. In addition to being inducted into the World Golf Hall of Fame in 1974, Nicklaus was honored with the title of PGA Player of the Year on five separate occasions (1967, 1972, 1973, 1975, and 1976). In 1990, he became a member of the Senior PGA Tour, which was subsequently renamed the Champions Tour. In 2005, he concluded his career as a tournament golfer. His career includes 73 wins on the PGA Tour, which is a statistic that is only surpassed by Sam Snead and Tiger Woods. Additionally, he holds the record for the most victories in the four major professional tournaments, with 18. In addition to having a huge amount of natural skill and power, Nicklaus displayed an extraordinary level of coolness even while under the most intense pressure from the competition.

Nicholas Nicklaus was responsible for the design of a number of golf courses, one of which being the Muirfield Village Golf Course in Ohio, which became the location of the Nicklaus-sponsored Memorial Tournament in 1976. Additionally, he is the author of a number of books, some of which are Golf My Way (1974), Nicklaus by Design (2002, written in collaboration with Chris Millard), and Jack Nicklaus: Memories and Mementos from Golf's Golden Bear (2007, written in collaboration with David Shedloski). Nicholas Nicklaus was presented with the Presidential Medal of Freedom in 2005.

73

NEYMAR JR. (SOCCER)

Brazilian football (soccer) player Neymar is among the all-time leading scorers for his legendary national team. He was born on February 5, 1992, in Mogi das Cruzes.

As a young kid in São Vicente, Neymar started playing football with the help of his father, a former professional player who was heavily involved in his son's career as a coach and mentor. After participating in both outdoor and indoor five-a-side football, Neymar became a member of the youth squad in São Vicente for Portuguesa Santista. In 2003, he and his family relocated to Santos. Already a talented player, Neymar enrolled at Santos FC's youth academy in Brazil—the same club where Pelé spent much of his domestic career. Santos had to up their expenditure to keep him after he had a good trial with Real Madrid of Spain when he was only 14 years old.

With a slim build, explosive speed, lightning reflexes, and great body control, 5-foot-9-inch (1.75-meter) striker Neymar had an air of absolute self-assurance on the pitch. With Santos, he debuted in a professional league game in 2009. He helped Santos win the Libertadores Cup in 2011—the most prestigious club championship in South America—while playing for the club, averaging a goal per match. While playing for Santos, Neymar won several individual accolades, one of which was South American Footballer of the Year in 2011 and 2012.

After becoming one of the most expensive football transfers ever in a deal with Santos for €57 million (approximately $76 million), Neymar signed a five-year contract with FC Barcelona in June 2013. Two years down the road, he was an integral part of Barcelona's "treble" of La Liga, Copa del Rey, and UEFA Champions League glory. As a key player in Barcelona's 2013–2017 triumph, Neymar scored 105 goals in 186 club appearances across all competitions. However, he yearned to emerge from the shadow of legendary colleague Lionel Messi. So, he arranged for a record-breaking €222 million ($263 million) move to Paris Saint-Germain (PSG), a French club, in August 2017. With an annual salary of €45 million ($53 million), Neymar became the highest-paid player in the world at the time as a result of the transfer. In August 2017, PSG also acquired Kylian Mbappé. In his first season at PSG, Neymar scored 28 goals in 30 appearances before fracturing a bone in his right foot. Despite this, PSG won the Ligue 1 championship in 2017–18, 2018–19, and 2019–20. Along with Messi's signing with PSG in 2021, Neymar extended his contract with the club, tying him to the club until 2025. A trio of Neymar, Mbappé, and Messi emerged as one of football's most dangerous attacking trios.

On the international stage, Neymar came near selection for Brazil's 2010 World Cup team in South Africa, but he was eventually left out. In fact, he didn't make his official debut until August of 2010—a friendly match against the United States—in which he scored Brazil's first international goal in a 2-0 victory. In 2013, he was Brazil's most useful player at the Confederations Cup, with four goals—including one in the final 3-0 win against Spain—and he also finished third in scoring, earning him the Bronze Boot and the Golden Ball. Brazil hosted the 2014 World Cup, and Neymar was a standout player for the host nation. He scored four goals in five games before suffering a broken vertebra that eliminated him in the quarterfinals. Brazil was stunned by eventual winner Germany's 7-1 semifinal victory despite being without their star player. Neymar was named the tournament's most valuable player despite leaving the competition early. With his game-winning penalty kick in the overtime thriller against Germany at the 2016 Summer Olympics in Rio de Janeiro, he helped propel Brazil's men's national team to its first-ever Olympic gold medal.

74

LEWIS HAMILTON (FORMULA 1)

One of the all-time greats in Formula One (F1) Grand Prix racing is Lewis Hamilton, a British race car driver born on January 7, 1985, in Stevenage, England. He has won more Formula One races than anybody else in his career and is tied with Michael Schumacher for second place in drivers' championships with seven. He broke racial barriers in 2008 by becoming the first Black driver to win the Formula One world championship.

Hamilton got his start behind the wheel at the tender age of eight. At age 10, he took home the trophy in the British Kart Championship. Hamilton was signed to the Young Driver Support Programme by McLaren and Mercedes-Benz three years later, where he received the support and assistance he needed to practice and hone his abilities. After being the youngest driver to ever hold the number one spot in the sport at the tender age of fifteen, he went on to win the European and global karting championships from 1998 to 2000.

Hamilton went on to compete in motor races, eventually winning 10 of the 15 races he contested in 2003 to claim the title of British Formula Renault series champion. The Formula Three Euroseries championship was his focus the year after. In 2005, he took home the championship. The following year, he went on to win the GP2 (Grand Prix 2) title in only one season with a team that competed in the series, which was meant to assist drivers get ready for F1.

The McLaren Formula One team welcomed Hamilton in 2007. In his first year on the circuit, he finished second in the drivers' championship, behind only Kimi Räikkönen of Finland by a single point. In that year, he equaled Jacques Villeneuve for most wins by a rookie in Formula One with four triumphs. He won five races the next year when he was 23 years old, and he won the driver's championship. (Until Sebastian Vettel won it in 2010, Hamilton was the youngest person to ever take the title.)

In Hamilton's following seasons with McLaren, he remained a prominent F1 driver, winning two races in 2009, three in 2010, and four in 2012. Hamilton joined the Mercedes-Benz Formula One team in September 2012 after deciding to leave McLaren. Although he struggled to adapt in his first season with Mercedes-Benz and won only one race in 2013, Hamilton nevertheless amassed enough points to finish in the top five of the drivers' championship standings for seven seasons in a row.

In 2014, Hamilton had a dominant season in Formula One, winning 11 races—a record for him—and clinching his second driver's title. Just one month before the 2015 season came to a close, he won his third driver's title, demonstrating his continued dominance. Mercedes-Benz won the Formula One constructor's title in both seasons thanks to Hamilton and Nico Rosberg's performances. Hamilton finished second in the drivers' standings in 2016, behind his teammate Rosberg, while Mercedes-Benz claimed the championships. Hamilton won his fourth driver's title the next year with nine race victories. With his fifth driver's title in 2018, he is now tied with Juan Manuel Fangio for second all-time in Formula One history. Hamilton finished one title behind Michael Schumacher the following year after winning his sixth drivers' championship. As he broke Schumacher's record for most career Formula One races won (91) in 2020, Hamilton equaled him for the most championships with seven.

75

FLOYD MAYWEATHER JR (BOXING)

One of the greatest pound-for-pound boxers of all time was Floyd Mayweather, Jr., an American boxer who was born on February 24, 1977, in Grand Rapids, Michigan. Mayweather had exceptional speed, power, and technical skill.

In his amateur days, Mayweather was known as "Pretty Boy" because of the lack of facial markings he wore. His amateur career came to a disappointing end in the semi-finals of the 1996 Olympic Games in Atlanta, when he lost by a disputed decision to Bulgarian Serafim Todorov and had to settle for bronze in the featherweight class. He had previously won the national Golden Gloves in 1993, 1994, and 1996. After knocking off American Roberto Apodaca in the second round, he went professional on October 11, 1996. On October 3, 1998, in his 18th fight, Mayweather won the WBC junior lightweight title by knocking out veteran American titleholder Genaro Hernandez in the eighth round. This came despite a bitter feud between his two trainers, Floyd Mayweather, Sr., and Roger

Mayweather, who had previously held the super featherweight (junior lightweight) and super lightweight (junior welterweight) titles held by the World Boxing Council (WBC). In 1998, Mayweather was again named Fighter of the Year by Ring magazine.

Mayweather successfully competed in four different weight classes, winning the lightweight and junior welterweight championships from the Ring magazine and the WBC in 2001, the super lightweight title from the WBC in 2005 (after defeating Arturo Gatti), and the welterweight belts from the Ring magazine and the WBC in 2006. With an unbeaten record of 38 fights (24 by knockout), he was already largely regarded as the world's top pound-for-pound fighter at the start of 2007. The public began to take notice of Mayweather after his victory against Oscar De La Hoya, another American, for the WBC super welterweight (junior middleweight) belt. More so than the bout itself, Mayweather's fame was elevated by the four-part documentary 24/7, which aired on HBO cable during the fight's buildup. He developed into an interesting protagonist with a flair for both annoying and endearing moments and an ego that matched his skill. Pay-per-view and live-gate sales for Mayweather vs. De La Hoya shattered previous records. He made his boxing comeback in December 2007 and knocked out Ricky Hatton, a previously unbeaten British fighter, in the tenth round in Las Vegas. Along with his triumph against De La Hoya, Mayweather was named Fighter of the Year for that year by Ring magazine, and the fight drew yet another sold-out audience.

Mayweather announced his retirement from boxing in June 2008, months before his anticipated rematch with De La Hoya. Despite the widespread belief that Mayweather's "retirement" would be short-lived, the 18-month gap between his fights with Hatton and Juan Manuel Márquez—a natural lightweight and fan favorite who agreed to face Mayweather in September 2009—was everything but. After 12 rounds, the judges unanimously decided in favor of Mayweather, despite Márquez's impressive resilience.

The buildup to Mayweather's next fight, which was supposed to be against Filipino sensation Manny Pacquiao, was filled with drama and a touch of gamesmanship. Pacquiao was accused of using performance-enhancing drugs by Mayweather's father, which caused a long squabble over the type of blood testing that would be conducted before the fight. In a nontitle fight in May of 2010, Mayweather defeated three-time welterweight champion Shane Mosley by majority decision while the Pacquiao match was on hold. Mayweather faced Victor Ortiz again in September 2011, reclaiming the WBC welterweight championship he had given up when he retired. Ortiz had come up to him to apologies for a previous head butt, and Mayweather controversially (albeit lawfully) knocked him out.

76

MANNY PACQUIAO (BOXING)

American politician, media personality, and world-renowned boxer Manny Pacquiao was born on December 17, 1978, in Kibawe, Bukidnon province, Mindanao, Philippines. He became famous for winning more weight classes than any other boxer in history. His extraordinary journey from extreme poverty to the highest level of his sport is further highlighted by his extraordinary life outside of the ring. Commercial endorsements, films, TV series, CDs, and even a postage stamp featuring the charismatic 'Pac-Man' were all products of the Philippines, where he was a national hero and a uniting force.

While still a youngster, Pacquiao hid aboard a ship heading to Manila, where he trained for a career in boxing. On January 22, 1995, at the tender age of 16, he made his professional boxing debut in the junior flyweight division. He became a fan favorite among Filipino boxing fans because of his all-action style and boyish grin, which were featured in many of his early fights that aired on Blow by Blow. On December

4, 1998, he defeated Chatchai Sasakul of Thailand by knockout to win the flyweight championship from the World Boxing Council (WBC). This was his first big title victory. But in September 1999, he lost the championship to Thai competitor Medgoen Singsurat when he failed to gain weight. In his debut fight in the US, Pacquiao knocked out Lehlo Ledwaba in the sixth round to win the IBF junior featherweight championship on June 23, 2001. This was Pacquiao's move-up in the weight class. After successfully defending his featherweight title four times, he finally became the champion on November 15, 2003, by knocking out Marco Antonio Barrera of Mexico.

Pacquiao won the featherweight championships of the World Boxing Association (WBA) and the International Boxing Federation (IBF), as well as the junior lightweight titles of the World Boxing Council (WBC) and The Ring, and the lightweight title of the WBC, in a string of high-profile bouts in the years that followed. American trainer Freddie Roach helped him reach to the top of the boxing world by bringing out the best in the left-handed power puncher without watering down his inherent aggressiveness or hitting strength. He won the titles of Fighter of the Year in 2006 and 2008 from The Ring and the Boxing Writers Association of America.

The legendary nontitle welterweight contest between Pacquiao and Oscar De La Hoya took place in Las Vegas on December 6, 2008, and Pacquiao dominated the fight. It was at this point that Pacquiao was generally believed to be the best boxer in the world, pound for pound, because of his improved defense, lightning speed, and impeccable footwork. Furthermore, Pacquiao's PPV boxing stardom had been on the rise since 2002, but his bout with De La Hoya was the catalyst that launched him into the international spotlight. One of the highest pay-per-view earnings ever for a nonheavyweight fight, with 1.25 million buys and around $70 million in revenue.

With an impressive one-punch knockout of Ricky Hatton of England in the second round on May 2, 2009, Pacquiao became the junior welterweight title of The Ring. This was his sixth weight class as a champion and ninth in his professional boxing career. After beating Puerto Rican Miguel Cotto in 12 rounds to win the World Boxing Organization (WBO) welterweight title on November 14, he added another championship belt to his collection—in a record-breaking seventh weight class. Pacquiao successfully defended his championship in a 12-round bout against Joshua Clottey of Ghana on March 13, 2010, in Arlington, Texas. On November 13, 2010, Pacquiao beat Antonio Margarito, the WBC super welterweight champion and a 17-pound heavier opponent than Pacquiao, extending his record of weight-class championships to eight.

77

SIMONE BILES

Simone Biles, an American gymnast who was widely regarded as a legend, was born on March 14, 1997, in Columbus, Ohio, USA. Not only did she become the first gymnast to win three consecutive global all-around championships (2013–2015), but she also became the first female U.S. gymnast to capture four gold medals in a single Olympics in Rio de Janeiro in 2016.

After being adopted by their grandparents, Ronald and Nellie Biles, Biles and her sister Adria spent their childhood in Spring, Texas, which is part of the Houston metropolitan region. During a nursery field trip to Bannon's Gymnastics when Simone was six years old, she developed an interest in gymnastics; she continued to train there for eleven years with Aimee Boorman as her instructor. Prior to her 2011 promotion to the elite level, Biles won the Women's Junior Olympic National Championships in floor exercise (2010) and vault

(2010). A little under two years later, she was unrivalled in her field. Her routines on the vault, uneven bars, balancing beam, and floor exercise were very tough, and Biles was consistently outstanding. Her enthusiastic nature and high level of difficulty also contributed to her standing out.

The 4-foot-9-inch (1.45-meter) Biles became the first African American woman to win the all-around title at the 2013 World Gymnastics Championships, which she competed in during her first year as a senior athlete. On top of it, she won bronze in balancing beam, silver in vault, and the floor exercise. Biles won four gold medals at the 2014 World Championships: one for the women's team and one each for the individual all-around, balancing beam, and floor exercise events. In the vault, she again won the silver medal.

In 2015, Biles became the first woman since Kim Zmeskal in 1992 to win the U.S. all-around event for the third year in a row. She won her third consecutive all-around win at the 2015 World Championships. In addition to her team triumph, she won bronze in vault, floor exercise, and balancing beam, and she shared the title with her teammates. Her 14 medals in the world championships are the most ever won by a gymnast from the United States, regardless of gender. Furthermore, no female gymnast had ever earned more than her record-setting ten gold medals from the world championships.

Even though she didn't meet the age requirement to compete in the 2012 London Olympics, Biles was a heavy favorite heading into the 2016 Rio de Janeiro Games. As predicted, she helped the U.S. win gold in the team event and went on to win the individual all-around. Becoming the sixth female gymnast to win four gold medals at the same Olympics, she also won the floor and vault competitions. With her bronze on the balance beam, Biles now has five medals in her collection. Following her time away from gymnastics, she came clean in 2018 about her experiences as a victim of Larry Nassar, a doctor who had been convicted of sexually assaulting several athletes and had worked as a doctor for the United States national gymnastics team. Biles went back to competing that year. In 2018, she made a new record in the U.S. national championships by becoming the first female gymnast in over 25 years to win all five events, including the all-around. By adding four golds (including an additional all-around title), one silver, and one bronze to her career total of 20 medals in the 2018 championships, Biles became the most decorated female gymnast in the history of world championships.

78

DAVID BECKHAM (SOCCER)

English football (soccer) player David Beckham came to popularity both on and off the pitch, thanks to his well-publicized personal life and his birth on May 2, 1975, in Leytonstone, East London, England.

Beckham won a football tournament when he was eleven years old, and he was a key member of Manchester United's youth team that won the national title in 1992 when he was a teenager. He didn't make his professional team debut until after three years; he was an integral part of Manchester United's 1995–96 league and FA Cup championship teams. In August 1996, Beckham became a household name after scoring a goal from the halfway line, which is similar to a golfer's hole-in-one. United successfully defended their league championship the next year, and Beckham was named the league's best young player. Manchester United won the league, FA Cup, and European Cup in 1998–99. Beckham took home the hardware for the top midfielder and MVP. Among the sport's all-time greats, he was most famous for his spectacular free kicks and crosses, which were featured prominently in the 2002 biopic Bend It Like Beckham. He was a key member of Manchester United's championship teams in 2000, 2001, and 2003 before leaving for Real Madrid of Spain in 2003. After waiting four years, he inked a record-breaking contract with the American soccer team Los Angeles Galaxy of the Major League Soccer (MLS). Beckham joined AC Milan, a footballing behemoth in Italy, in October 2008 during the 2008 Major League Soccer offseason. The Galaxy won the MLS Cup in 2011 with his aid. After the 2012 season, in which the Galaxy won their second MLS Cup, Beckham decided to leave the club. He signed with Paris Saint-Germain (PSG), a first-league club in France, in 2013, and during his one season there, PSG won the French domestic championship. After Beckham and PSG won the title, he quickly decided to retire from the sport.

In a 1996 World Cup qualifying match, Beckham made his international debut for England. His ejection from a match in 1998 for kicking an opponent garnered a lot of criticism. England was knocked out of the tournament after losing the match. Beckham was appointed captain of the national squad in 2000. The quarterfinals were the end for England in both the 2002 and 2006 World Cups. Beckham was relieved of his captaincy and subsequently benched by England after the 2006 competition. After being recalled to the squad in 2007, he became the sixth English footballer to reach 100 appearances for his country the following year. In March of 2010, while playing for AC Milan, Beckham tore his Achilles tendon, which prevented him from making an appearance in the 2010 World Cup. He was on track to become the first Englishman to do so. Beckham played 115 appearances for England, the most ever for a non-goalkeeper, yet despite being healthier and older, he was not chosen to represent England in the 2012 European Championship.

Even after his playing days were over, Beckham kept busy with football. Notably, he launched the Inter Miami CF Major League Soccer franchise in 2020 as both owner and president.

79

JAMES HARDEN (BASKETBALL)

James Harden (born August 26, 1989, in Los Angeles, California, U.S.) is one of the finest NBA shooting guards and popularized a three-point shot that changed the sport. Harden won three scoring championships and was voted NBA MVP in 2018. The Los Angeles Clippers are his current team after playing for the Oklahoma City Thunder, Houston Rockets, Brooklyn Nets, and Philadelphia 76ers.

Harden was born in Los Angeles to Monja Willis and James Harden, Sr., but was raised by his mother. Including a sister and half-brother, the family resided in Compton, California. Harden concentrated on baseball, playing first base and pitching. He discovered his passion for basketball at age ten while playing for a Watts recreational team. In his junior and senior years at Artesia High School in Lakewood, California, Harden averaged roughly 19 points per game and led the team to two state titles.

The University of Washington, the University of Arizona, and the University of California in Los Angeles recruited Harden. He joined ASU. He led the league in steals and averaged 17.8 points, 5.3 rebounds, and 3.2 assists as a rookie (2007–08). Harden made Pac-10 first and all-freshman teams. Harden improved the next season, averaging 20.1 points and 4.2 assists. He was Pac-10 Player of the Year and consensus All-American. Harden entered the NBA draft after the Sun Devils fell in the NCAA tournament's second round.

The Oklahoma City Thunder drafted Harden third overall. In his debut season (2009–10), he played 76 games off the bench and averaged 9.9 points. Harden finished the season on the All-Rookie second team. He played off the bench for two more seasons, with approximately 17 points, 3.7 assists, and 4.1 rebounds in 2011–12. The Thunder fell to the Miami Heat in five games in the NBA finals that season. Harden was awarded NBA Sixth Man of the Year, honoring the league's best bench player. He earned a London Olympics gold medal with the U.S. men's basketball team in 2012. Harden was famous for his play and his thick beard, which became his defining appearance.

Harden rejected Oklahoma City's four-year, $55 million contract deal in the summer. He was traded to the Houston Rockets before the 2012–13 season, who quickly signed him to a five-year, $80 million deal. Harden started after coming off the bench to be a key player. He earned his first NBA All-Star bid with 25.9 points per game for the Rockets. Houston reached the playoffs for the first time in four years but fell in the first round. In 2014–15, Harden averaged 27.4 points and seven assists, finishing second in MVP voting behind Stephen Curry. Despite little postseason success, the Harden-led Rockets were one of the league's best in the 2010s.

Harden earned his first MVP title in 2017–18 with 30.4 points and 8.8 assists per game. He earned the NBA scoring championship for the first time that season. He averaged 36.1 and 34.3 points per game in 2018–19 and 2019–20, respectively, continuing his hot run. In both seasons, he topped the league in scoring. His three-point shot, in which he steps back before launching, has helped Harden. Step-back three-pointers have grown popular in the sport, increasing the number of attempts made.

The Rockets had reached the playoffs every season under Harden, but they had never advanced beyond the Western Conference finals.

Harden demanded a move in 2020 and was sent to the Brooklyn Nets early in 2021. Despite hamstring concerns, Harden managed to score well in a restricted role. Despite their star-studded lineup, including Kevin Durant, the Nets underperformed in the playoffs, and Harden was dealt to the Philadelphia 76ers halfway through the 2021–22 season. Harden thrived in 2022–23 alongside Joel Embiid. After 10 consecutive selections, he missed his first All-Star squad but had a near-career-high 10.7 assists in his new supporting position. After a playoff defeat in the Eastern Conference semifinals, Harden sought a trade in August 2023 and was traded to the Clippers in October.

80

JOE MONTANA (FOOTBALL)

Joe Montana was born on June 11, 1956, in New Eagle, Pennsylvania. He played gridiron football and is widely considered one of the all-time best quarterbacks in NFL history. Montana was selected Super Bowl MVP three times while leading the San Francisco 49ers to four championships (1982, 1985, 1989, 1990). He has 273 touchdown passes and 40,551 passing yards, both of which place him among football's all-time greats. Montana earned the moniker "Joe Cool" for his cool demeanour in the last seconds of games when his side was down and out.

Montana was an all-star in football, basketball, and baseball while growing up in Monongahela, Pennsylvania. He turned down a basketball scholarship from Raleigh, North Carolina's North Carolina State University, in favor of a football scholarship from South Bend, Indiana's University of Notre Dame. In 1977, when he was a junior, Montana was the Fighting Irish's third-string quarterback. However, he was promoted to starting quarterback after leading a comeback win in Notre Dame's third game. At the end of that season, he led Notre Dame, a team that had previously lost, to the Division I-A national title. The 49ers picked Montana in the third round of the 1979 NFL draft after a great senior year that culminated with Notre Dame's Cotton Bowl triumph.

In the middle of his second season with the 49ers, Montana was promoted to starting quarterback. Bill Walsh's "West Coast offence," which let him make quick decisions and see the field well, was perfect for getting the ball down the field with a string of short, accurate passes. Montana was named the game's most valuable player in January 1982 after leading the 49ers to their first Super Bowl triumph. The play that culminated his team's playoff journey was "The Catch," the National Football Conference championship game-winning touchdown throw from Montana to Dwight Clark with 51 seconds left. In 1985, the 49ers defeated the Miami Dolphins in the Super Bowl, resulting in the 49ers' second victory and Montana's second MVP award. Jerry Rice was selected by the 49ers in the spring of the following year as a wide receiver. For six seasons, he and Montana formed one of the most successful throwing combos in NFL history. In 1989, Montana guided his team to a thrilling comeback victory against the Cincinnati Bengals in the Super Bowl, securing their third title. The 49ers won Super Bowl 50 by 45 points, the biggest margin of victory in the game's history, and Montana won his third MVP award despite losing Walsh to retirement during the offseason. Montana won the Most Valuable Player awards from the NFL in 1989 and 1990, in addition to his playoff honors.

When Montana returned to the field in 1992 after missing most of the 1991 and 1992 seasons due to an elbow injury, the 49ers had already solidified the starting quarterback position with Steve Young, who would go on to become a Hall of Famer. When the Kansas City Chiefs acquired Montana in 1993, it constituted a trade. In his first season with the Chiefs, he was selected to the Pro Bowl—his eighth and last selection in a career—and guided the club to playoff spots in each of his seasons there. In his eleven years as a starting quarterback for the NFL, Montana amassed 31 fourth-quarter comeback wins and made it to the playoffs ten times before retiring in 1995. In 2000, he was inducted into the Pro Football Hall of Fame.

81

PEYTON MANNING (FOOTBALL)

As one of the all-time greats in NFL quarterback history, Peyton Manning was born on March 24, 1976, in New Orleans, Louisiana, USA. He played gridiron football for both university and professional teams. While playing quarterback for the Denver Broncos (2016) and the Indianapolis Colts (2007), he was a Super Bowl champion.

The sport of football consumed Manning's life from an early age. The late Archie Manning was a superb quarterback for the Saints of the National Football League. (Eli, the younger brother, went on to become a quarterback in the National Football League and directed the New York Giants to Super Bowl XLII and XLVI victories.) Peyton Manning was named the national player of the year during his final year of high school and was widely considered a star athlete. His four years as a starting quarterback at UT were highlights of his college career. He was named to the first team All-American team in 1997 and concluded his undergraduate career in 1998 with more throwing yards than any other Titan. In 1996, he won the Sullivan Award for best amateur athlete in the nation.

In 1998, the Indianapolis Colts picked Manning with the first overall pick. Even though he had a rough rookie year, he was an integral part of the 1999 Colts team that won their first division championship since 1987. Manning was one of the NFL's top quarterbacks in 2000, with 4,413 yards and 33 touchdowns. Three years down the road, he and Tennessee Titans quarterback Steve McNair split the MVP honors. Despite having his single-season touchdown record broken in 2007 and his passer rating record dropped in 2011, Manning's 2004 performance—which featured 49 touchdown passes and a passer rating of 121.1—was exceptional enough to earn him the MVP accolade outright. His charming attitude and exceptional play on the pitch made him a huge hit as a commercial pitchman, catapulting him to stardom. Few football players—whose accessibility to fans has historically been limited by factors like the briefness of their careers and playing while wearing face-obscuring helmets—had ever achieved the level of fame that Manning did, even though he was not as seemingly omnipresent as modern athletes like Michael Jordan and Tiger Woods.

Manning led the 2005 Indianapolis Colts to a 13–game winning streak. It was a divisional playoff loss to the Pittsburgh Steelers despite being a heavy favorite to win the Super Bowl. Manning put his detractors to rest in 2006 after they doubted his ability to lead the team to a title. In leading the Colts to 12 regular season victories, he threw for 4,397 yards, surpassing Dan Marino's record and became the eighth player in his career to do so. After sweeping the Chiefs, Ravens, and Patriots in the playoffs, Manning led the Colts to a Super Bowl XLI victory against the Bears. Manning was selected the game's most valuable player for his effort, which included 25 completions for 247 yards. He had a franchise-best 14-0 start with the Colts in 2009 on his way to a record-breaking fourth MVP title; in 2008, he earned the league MVP award a record three times. With another game-changing interception in the fourth quarter of the Colts' defeat to the Saints, Manning brought back the ghost of his previous inability to win important games, even though he guided the team to another Super Bowl appearance the following playoffs.

82

BRETT FAVRE (FOOTBALL)

Brett Favre, an American gridiron football player who played for the Green Bay Packers and set several NFL throwing records throughout his career, was born on October 10, 1969, in Gulfport, Mississippi, USA.

When Favre was a freshman at the University of Southern Mississippi, he took over as starting quarterback for the football team. He was born and raised in Kiln, Mississippi. After the Atlanta Falcons picked him in 1991, he was moved to Green Bay the following year due to his falling out of favor with the coaching staff in Atlanta. After starting the third game of the 1992 season in place of an injured colleague, he never again played the role of backup quarterback. Favre became one of the best quarterbacks in NFL history in 1993, the year he also led the Packers to their first playoff berth in ten years. He was the league's leading passer in touchdown passes in each of the three years he was MVP (1995, 1996, and 1997) and was famous for his speed, intensity, and presence on the field.

Favre led the Green Bay Packers to a Super Bowl XXXI triumph against the New England Patriots at the conclusion of the 1996 season. When he went back to the Super Bowl the next year, it was with the Green Bay Packers, but they were defeated in the last seconds by John Elway's Denver Broncos. In the years after their two trips to the Super Bowl, the Packers had less success, but Favre kept producing quality quarterback work. Not only did he top the league in passing yards in 1998 and touchdown passes in 2003, but he also led the league in pass completions in 1998 and 2005. Throughout the years 1992–2007, he was a top-10 passer in every category (completions, passing yards, and touchdown passes). Throughout his career, Favre accomplished unparalleled individual statistical achievements in addition to these single-season accolades. He shattered many records in 2007—Elway's record of 148 career starts as a quarterback, Dan Marino's record of 420 touchdown passes and 61,371 passing yards, and George Blanda's record of 277 interceptions. At the conclusion of the 2007 NFL season, Favre announced his retirement from professional football.

The NFL reinstated Favre the month after he made his intentions clear in July 2008 to return to the league. Before the 2008 NFL season began, however, the Packers traded him to the New York Jets due to his troubled relationship with Packers management and the team's dedication to a new starting quarterback. Despite Favre being nominated to his tenth Pro Bowl in 2008, his one season with the Jets was nevertheless underwhelming. After getting out to an 8-3 start, the Jets only managed to win nine games and failed to make it to the playoffs, even though he topped the league in interceptions and finished 21st in passer rating. Once again, Favre announced his retirement in February 2009, this time citing diminishing playing abilities and an injured biceps. After weeks of publicly declaring his intention not to return, Favre signed with the Minnesota Vikings in August 2009, putting an end to speculation that he might terminate his second retirement as the NFL season drew closer.

With a record-low seven interceptions and a completion percentage and passer rating that all surpassed his previous bests, Favre enjoyed a breakout season in 2009. The Vikings reached the NFC title game because of his leadership and a 12–4 record. His incredible season came to an abrupt end, however, as he threw an interception in the final seconds, allowing the New Orleans Saints to win the NFC title in overtime when the Vikings were within striking distance of a game-winning field goal attempt. In 2010, Favre missed the thirteenth game due to a serious shoulder injury; he had previously started 297 straight regular-season games, which was a record for longevity in his position, and he retired for the third time that season. After Favre's career, Peyton Manning surpassed the marks he had set by Favre with 71,838 throwing yards and 508 touchdown passes. The 2016 Pro Football Hall of Fame class included Favre.

83

EMMITT SMITH (FOOTBALL)

American gridiron football player Emmitt Smith, who was born on May 15, 1969, in Pensacola, Florida, United States, became the all-time top rusher in the history of the National Football League (NFL) in the year 2002 after his accomplishments. After finishing the 2004 season with 18,355 yards running, he decided to retire. He also holds the record for the most touchdowns scored on the ground in a career, with 164 scored.

Smith began his football career with great success, going on to become a star in youth leagues, and by the time he graduated from high school, he had already been recognized as the national Player of the Year by Parade magazine and other publications. Before being taken by the Dallas Cowboys in the first round of the 1990 NFL draft, he played for three years (1987–1989) at the University of Florida (in Gainesville), where he set 58 school records during his time there. In a short amount of time, Smith became recognized as one of the most talented running backs in the league. In 1990, he was honored as the NFL Offensive Rookie of the Year. The next year, he ran for 1,563 yards, which earned him the first of his four NFL rushing crowns (the other three were in 1992–1993, 1995, and 1995). Smith was a member of a dangerous Dallas offence that included quarterback Troy Aikman and wide receiver Michael Irvin. This offence was instrumental in the Cowboys' four consecutive Super Bowl victories against the Buffalo Bills, which occurred in 1993 and 1994. He finished the 1993 regular season with a staggering average of 5.3 yards per carry, which earned him the title of Most Valuable Player in the National Football League. He carried for 1,486 yards. In 1996, Smith was victorious in the Super Bowl for the third time. In the late 1990s, he started to see a decline in his running totals, and the Cowboys decided to release him following the 2002 playing season. After that, Smith signed with the Arizona Cardinals, where he finished his career with two seasons that were not very noteworthy.

Smith excelled in the National Football League by depending on his power, doggedness, and excellent training. Despite the fact that he was somewhat short—he stood just 1.75 meters (5 feet 9 inches) tall and weighed 96 kilograms (212 pounds)—and lacked remarkable speed, he was able to achieve success in the NFL. In the end, he proved to be one of the most durable players in the National Football League (NFL) at any position; between the years 1990 and 2002, he was only involved in two games that he did not start. Although he was selected for the Pro Bowl eight times throughout the course of his career, he was not admitted into the Pro Football Hall of Fame until the year 2010.

84

WALTER PAYTON (FOOTBALL)

Walter Payton was an American professional gridiron football player who was born on July 25, 1954, in Columbia, Mississippi, United States, and passed away on November 1, 1999, in Barrington, Illinois. He was a rushing back who was known for his production and durability, which made him one of the best running backs in the history of the game. After retiring in 1987, he was the most successful rusher in the history of the National Football League (NFL). He retained this record until 2002 when Emmitt Smith overtook him as the most successful rusher in NFL history.

In high school and while attending Jackson State University in Mississippi, Payton was a member of the football team. His pleasant attitude and elegant athleticism earned him the nickname "Sweetness" during his time in college. This nickname was given to him because of his athleticism. During his time at Jackson State, he was not only the starting running back, but he also sometimes kicked the ball. His four-year total of 464 points set a record for the National Collegiate Athletic

Association. He was selected by the Chicago Bears as the fourth overall pick in the National Football League draft, which took place in 1975. After leading the National Football League in running yards (1,852, a club record) and rushing touchdowns (14), Payton was selected for the first of his nine career Pro Bowls in his second season. In 1977, he was also awarded the Most Valuable Player award by the National Football League. Through his contributions, the Bears were able to achieve a record of 15–1 during the 1985 season and go on to win the Super Bowl for the first time in January of the following year. After the 1987 season, he decided to retire.

Payton was not only an exceptional rusher, but he was also a good blocker, pass receiver, and even at the quarterback position. However, he was most well-known for his pinball running style, in which he often avoided being tackled by players who were attempting to catch him. One of the factors that contributed to his endurance was the intense off-season training routine that he followed; during his career, he started more than 180 straight games. All of the NFL records that he established have since been broken, including the total career rushing yardage of 16,726 yards, the most combined career yards from scrimmage (rushing and pass receiving 21,264 yards), the most seasons with 1,000 or more yards rushing (10), the most yards gained in a single game (275 yards), the most games with 100 or more yards gained in a career (77), and the most career touchdowns earned by rushing (110).

In the year 1993, Payton was inducted into the Pro Football Hall of Fame, and in the year 1994, he was selected for the 75th Anniversary All-Time Team of the National Football League. One of the most prestigious awards in college football, the Walter Payton Award, is given out on a yearly basis to the player who is considered to be the best in the Football Championship Subdivision. It is believed that Payton, who was suffering from a rare liver ailment in his last year of life, was the one who sparked a national interest in organ donation.

85

LAWRENCE TAYLOR (FOOTBALL)

American gridiron footballer Lawrence Taylor, who was born on February 4, 1959, in Williamsburg, Virginia, USA, is widely regarded as one of the game's all-time great linebackers. He won Super Bowls after the 1986 and 1990 seasons while playing with the New York Giants in the NFL.

Despite waiting until eleventh grade to participate in organized football, Taylor went on to play outside linebacker for the Tar Heels while he was a defensive lineman for the Tar Heels. Taylor was selected as an All-American in 1980 for his exceptional performance as a linebacker; he stood at 6 feet 3 inches (1.91 meters) tall and weighed 240 pounds (109 kg).

The New York Giants picked Taylor, the second overall choice in the 1981 NFL draft when he joined the league. He was known for his strong, aggressive hits and had 9.5 QB sacks at the conclusion of his rookie season (an unofficial tally as the NFL didn't start keeping sack statistics until the following season). He repeated as both the league's Rookie and Defensive Player of the Year the following year. He was the second defensive player in NFL history to win Most Valuable Player in 1986, after leading the league with 20.5 sacks and leading the Giants to a Super Bowl XXI triumph against the Denver Broncos. In Super Bowl XXV, which took place in January 1991, Taylor and the Giants defeated the Buffalo Bills to win their second title.

Outside linebacker was once known as a "read and react" position; players in this position would wait for a play to unfold before taking action to prevent it, but Taylor changed all of that. With his speed and power, Taylor could create plays all over the field as an attacking linebacker. When it came to defense, he was the game-changer for his time. Over the course of his 13-year career, he appeared in 10 Pro Bowls and was selected All-Pro six times (1981–87 and 1981–1990 seasons, respectively). After the 1993 season, he left the NFL with a record of 1,088 tackles, 132.5 sacks (not including his first-year sacks), 33 forced fumbles, and nine interceptions. The Pro Football Hall of Fame inducted him in 1999.

Throughout and after his time as a football player, Taylor struggled with issues in his personal life. He failed a drug test in 1988, leading to his suspension from the NFL, and he battled a cocaine addiction. Three separate drug-related arrests occurred between 1996 and 1998. In 1998, he finished a recovery programme and then went on to become an actor. Cowritten with Steve Serby in 2003, LT: Over the Edge recounted Taylor's troubled history. After reportedly having sexual contact with a 16-year-old girl at a motel in Suffern, N.Y., he was arrested and charged with third-degree rape and solicitation of a prostitute in May 2010. After entering a guilty plea in January 2011 to two misdemeanour charges—sexual misconduct and patronizing a prostitute—he was handed a six-year probationary term.

86

BARRY SANDERS (FOOTBALL)

Barry Sanders was an American professional gridiron football player who was considered to be one of the game's most spectacular running backs. Sanders was born on July 16, 1968, in Wichita, Kansas, in the United States. Sanders led the National Football League (NFL) in running competition four times during his ten seasons with the Detroit Lions (1989–1998). He was also picked for the Pro Bowl each and every year during his career with the Lions. In 2004, he was honored with induction into the Pro Football Hall of Fame.

Sanders's modest size of 1.73 meters (5 feet 8 inches) inhibited coaches from playing him as a running back until the final five games of his senior year of high school. By that time, Sanders had already played running back. The astounding 1,417 yards that he gained, on the other hand, were sufficient to win him a football scholarship to attend Oklahoma State University (OSU). In 1988, Sanders was given the starting halfback position and went on to carry for 2,628 yards, which was the finest single-season rushing performance in the history of the National Collegiate Athletic Association. As a result, he was awarded the Heisman Trophy that year, which is given to outstanding college football players in the United States. Sanders declared himself eligible for the professional draft the following year when Ohio State was placed on probation. The Detroit Lions picked him with the third overall choice in the draft when they made their selection.

The marks that Sanders established include running for more than one thousand yards in ten consecutive seasons, rushing for one thousand five hundred yards or more in five separate seasons (and becoming the first player to do it in four consecutive seasons), and rushing for more than one hundred yards in fourteen consecutive games. He became just the third running back in history to carry for more than 2,000 yards in 1997, which was his most spectacular season. He established a single-season record for running backs with 2,053 yards rushing and 305 yards in pass catches, which resulted in a total of 2,358 yards.

Sanders, much like Jim Brown, quit the game at or near the culmination of his athletic career. Sanders came quite close to surpassing Walter Payton's all-time records for running yards and touchdowns with 15,269 and 99, respectively, during the course of his career. In its place, Sanders was compelled to give back to the Detroit Lions more than five million dollars of his most recent signing bonus when he decided to retire earlier than expected.

87

DAN MARINO (FOOTBALL)

Dan Marino was an American gridiron football quarterback who established himself as one of the most prolific passers in the history of the National Football League (NFL). Marino was born on September 15, 1961, in Pittsburgh, Pennsylvania, in the United States.

He established himself as another of the great quarterbacks to come from western Pennsylvania, among such luminaries as Johnny Unitas, Joe Montana, and Joe Namath. Marino was a high school All-American in Pittsburgh, where he established himself as a quarterback like those mentioned above. Marino, in contrast to other quarterbacks, chose to remain in his hometown and play college football at the University of Pittsburgh, where he attained All-American status during his junior year. At the conclusion of the first round of the 1983 National Football League draft, Marino was selected by the Miami Dolphins. This was due to the fact that his senior season was not as successful as he had hoped it would be.

Instantaneous returns were obtained from Miami's investment. Six games into his first season, Marino was given the opportunity to take over as the starting quarterback for the club. After that, he was selected for the Pro Bowl and led the Dolphins to a playoff spot in the playoffs. In 1984, he made history by being the first quarterback to throw for more than 5,000 yards in a single season (5,084) and the first to complete more than 40 touchdown passes in a season (48). His records were subsequently beaten by Drew Brees and Peyton Manning, respectively. Marino was honored as the Most Valuable Player of the National Football League, and at the conclusion of that season, he made his one and only appearance in the Super Bowl of his career. Unfortunately, the Dolphins were defeated by Montana and the San Francisco 49ers in that game.

While he was in the National Football League, he topped the league in passing yards on four further occasions (1985, 1986, 1988, and 1992), and he also led the league in touchdown passes on two other occasions (1985 and 1986). Between 1985 and 1992, Marino and the Dolphins made it to the conference title game. However, throughout his 17-year career, Miami never made it any farther than that point in the playoffs. Marino was one of the most dominant players in his position despite the fact that his teams did not have the same level of success as those of other elite quarterbacks. By the time he finished his final season (1999), he had established all-time records for a variety of categories, including passes completed (4,453 in 7,452 attempts), yards passing (55,416), touchdown passes (385), and a number of other categories. Over the course of his career, Brett Favre was able to surpass Marino's most notable achievements.

Over the course of his career, both before and after he retired, he was a well-liked salesperson for a variety of items. Following his retirement from the sport, he began working as a football pundit on television until 2014, when he became a member of the front office staff of the Dolphins. Marino, who was selected for the All-Pro team three times and was honored with a Pro Bowl selection nine times, was inducted into the Pro Football Hall of Fame in 2005.

88

STEVE YOUNG (FOOTBALL)

Steve Young is an American gridiron football player who was born on October 11, 1961, in Salt Lake City, Utah, United States. He is widely regarded as one of the most accurate quarterbacks in the history of the National Football League (NFL).

Born and bred in Connecticut, Young attended Greenwich High School, where he excelled in both football and baseball, earning him all-state honors. His great-great-great-grandfather, Brigham Young, was an early leader in the Mormon faith. He went on to attend Brigham Young University, where he received his law degree in 1994. He was the great-great-great-grandson of Brigham Young. Young established thirteen national college records, one of which was his completion % of.713 in 1983, the year when he was recognized as one of the best five student-athletes in the United States.

Young chose a $40 million agreement with the Los Angeles Express of the United States Football League (USFL), which at the time was the largest contract in the history of team sports. The Cincinnati Bengals had the intention of selecting Young as the first choice in the 1984 NFL draft; however, Young rejected the offer and instead signed with the Los Angeles Express. It was only during his two seasons with a poor club that he was able to complete 56.4% of his throws while also throwing 16 touchdown passes and 22 interceptions. Following the conclusion of the spring season in 1985, he bought out his contract with the Express; nevertheless, his National Football League rights were held by the similarly unfortunate Tampa Bay Buccaneers. Young had a completion percentage of Five hundred thirty-three during his two seasons there, and he threw 11 touchdown passes while also throwing 21 interceptions.

As a backup quarterback for Joe Montana, who would go on to become a Hall of Famer in the National Football League, Young was transferred to the San Francisco 49ers in 1987. Young was given the opportunity to take over as the starting quarterback for the 49ers in 1991 when Montana was sidelined with an elbow injury. The National Football League (NFL) passed the most passes from 1991 to 1994, and Young was named the league's most valuable player (MVP) in both 1992 and 1994. At the end of the 1994 season, he concluded with a passer rating of 112.8, which was a number he obtained on a scale where 100 was supposed to be the most realistic possible. Additionally, he was the leader in the league in terms of yards per throw attempt, with an average gain of 8.7 yards for each and every pass that he attempted. This unprecedented run was brought to a close by his leadership of the 49ers in Super Bowl XXIX, which took place in 1995 and was won by the San Diego Chargers. In a performance that won him the title of Most Valuable Player of the game, Young established a new record by throwing six touchdown passes while completing 24 of 36 passes.

Young led the club to the National Football Conference (NFC) title game in 1997, and two years later, he was picked to play in the Pro Bowl for the seventh time. Young had a career passer rating of 96.8 at the time of his retirement in 1999. His later career included working as a motivational speaker in addition to his role as an analyst for a number of different sports programmes. In 2005, he was honored with induction into the Pro Football Hall of Fame. In 2016, Young's autobiography, titled QB: My Life Behind the Spiral, which was authored in collaboration with Jeff Benedict, was released.

89

FRANCO HARRIS (FOOTBALL)

Franco Harris was an American gridiron football running back who was born on March 7, 1950, in Fort Dix, New Jersey, United States, and passed away on December 21, 2022. He was a member of four teams that won the Super Bowl while playing for the Pittsburgh Steelers (1975, 1976, 1979, 1980). However, he is most well-known for his participation in "the Immaculate Reception," which is widely considered to be the most famous play in the history of the National Football League (NFL).

When Harris was a senior in high school, he excelled in the sports of baseball, basketball, and football. In 1968, he was awarded a football scholarship to attend Pennsylvania State University (often referred to as Penn State). During his time at Penn State, Harris was sometimes overshadowed by teammate running back Lydell Mitchell, who was an All-American. Despite this, Steelers scouts evaluated Harris's performance to the point that they selected him with the thirteenth overall pick in the 1972 NFL draft. After rushing for 1,055 yards and scoring ten touchdowns in his rookie year in the league, he was selected for the first of nine straight Pro Bowls and was awarded the title of Offensive Rookie of the Year. During that season, the Pittsburgh Steelers made it to the playoffs for the first time in twenty-five years. The game that they played against the Oakland Raiders in the first round was highlighted by Harris's game-winning shoestring grab, which became known as the Immaculate Reception. It was 22 seconds left in the game when the play took place, and the Steelers were on the losing end of a 7–6 deficit. Terry Bradshaw, the quarterback for the Steelers, attempted to throw a pass on fourth-and-10 from the Steelers' 40-yard line. However, the pass was knocked towards the ground by a Raider defender, and Harris emerged apparently out of nowhere to grab the ball and go into the end zone. In spite of the fact that the play raised a lot of controversy—some observers believe that the ball either hit the ground before Harris caught it or was deflected by another Pittsburgh player instead of the Oakland defender, which was against the rules at the time—it was still ruled a touchdown, and the Steelers ended up winning the game.

Not only did Harris have a string of eight consecutive appearances in the Pro Bowl, but he also helped the Steelers to eight consecutive playoff spots beginning in 1972, four of which were Super Bowl championships. After running for 158 yards against a formidable Minnesota Vikings defense in Super Bowl IX (1975), he was awarded the title of Most Valuable Player of the Tournament. He was a massive running back on account of his height of 6 feet 2 inches (1.88 meters) and his weight of 230 pounds (104 kilograms). However, he was sometimes criticized for being "soft" due to the fact that he had a propensity to avoid contact that he considered to be unnecessary by sprinting out of bounds. His conservative running technique, on the other hand, resulted in a lengthy career: he played for the Steelers for a total of twelve seasons and then for the Seattle Seahawks for an additional season. He finished his career with the third-greatest number of running yards in the history of the National Football League (NFL) when he retired in 1984. In 1990, Harris was honored with induction into the Pro Football Hall of Fame. In the year 2022, he passed away, only two days before the fifty-year anniversary of the play that brought him widespread recognition.

90

TERRY BRADSHAW (FOOTBALL)

Terry Bradshaw is an American professional gridiron football quarterback who was born on September 2, 1948, in Shreveport, Louisiana, United States. He is most known for his leadership of the Pittsburgh Steelers throughout the course of four Super Bowl titles (1975, 1976, 1979, and 1980).

Despite the fact that he was a highly valued college football recruit coming out of high school, Bradshaw chose to attend Louisiana Tech University in Ruston, which is located just around 70 miles (113 km) away from his hometown. This decision was made since Louisiana State University is a historic powerhouse among universities. All of the main school passing records were broken during his four years at Louisiana Tech, and the Steelers picked him with the first overall pick in the 1970 National Football League (NFL) draft. He went on to become the most successful quarterback in the history of the school. Once Bradshaw had completed his second season with the Pittsburgh Steelers, he was promoted to the position of starting quarterback on a full-time basis. In 1972, he led the club to its first of eight straight berths in the playoffs. Despite the fact that the well-balanced squad was one of the most successful in the league, Bradshaw struggled with his throwing accuracy and was relegated to the position of backup quarterback at the beginning of the 1974 season with the club. Over the course of the season, he worked his way back into the starting lineup, and in January of the following year, he led the Steelers to their first Super Bowl victory.

Bradshaw, who was firmly established as the quarterback for the Steelers, led the club to success in 1976 when they won their second championship in a row. As a result of his league-high 28 touchdown passes in 1978, he was awarded the title of Most Valuable Player (MVP) by the National Football League. As a result of his leadership throughout the upcoming playoffs, the Steelers were able to secure another Super Bowl triumph, and Bradshaw was named the game's Most Valuable Player. His offence was so effective that it averaged 34 points per game. Once again, the team won the championship in 1980, and Bradshaw was honored with the title of Most Valuable Player of the Super Bowl for his performance. Following his retirement at the conclusion of the 1983 season, he was included in the Pro Football Hall of Fame in 1989.

Bradshaw went on to become a popular television football pundit once he concluded his playing career. Additionally, he was a successful performer in the fields of gospel and country music, and he appeared in a number of films and television shows. The reality television series The Bradshaw Bunch (2020–) focuses on his family as its primary subject matter. The book It's Only a Game, which was written by Bradshaw in collaboration with David Fisher and published in 2001, details Bradshaw's life from his childhood to his post-football activities.

91

RANDY MOSS (FOOTBALL)

Randy Moss is a professional gridiron football player from the United States who was born on February 13, 1977, in Rand, West Virginia. He is widely regarded as one of the best wide receivers in NFL history.

Despite Moss's stellar performance on the football and basketball fields in high school, the University of Notre Dame withdrew its scholarship offer when he was arrested for violence during his senior year. He was expelled from the school's football team after failing a drug test, which was a violation of his parole, shortly after he started at Florida State University. He took a scholarship to play football at Marshall University in Division I-AA (now the Football Championship Subdivision) after exhausting all other possibilities to play for a top-tier collegiate programme. During his rookie year, Moss helped lead Marshall to a national title while setting many marks for receiving in the I-AA. After moving up to Division I-A (now the Football Bowl Subdivision) in his second year, Marshall had Moss established an I-A record with 25 touchdown receptions. The Minnesota Vikings waited until the 21st choice of the first round (despite Moss's widespread reputation as one of the most gifted players available) to choose him in the 1998 NFL draft due to concerns over his character.

Upon joining the Vikings, Moss became an instant star. At the highest level of football, Moss's combination of astonishing speed, a stocky 6-foot-4-inch (1.93-meter) build, and exceptional jumping ability perplexed opponents just as much as it did in high school and college when he had earned the moniker "The Freak" at Marshall. He was voted the NFL Offensive Rookie of the Year, established a rookie record with 17 receiving touchdowns, and was chosen to be on the first team of All-Pro players. With a 15-1 record before losing in the NFC title game, Minnesota set a new NFL record for most points scored in a season. Over the next two seasons, Moss continued his impressive career by catching at least 1,400 yards and 11 touchdown passes. In 2003, he established a new mark with 111 catches for 1,632 yards.

The Vikings sent Moss to the Raiders in a 2005 trade. By his standards, Moss's two seasons with the Raiders were fruitless; he was moved to the Patriots in 2007 after scoring a total of eleven touchdowns.

In New England, Moss swiftly reversed his professional trajectory. He was an integral part of the 2007 Patriots' offense, which set a new single-season scoring record and made them the first NFL team to go undefeated in a regular season when they were joined by quarterback Tom Brady. Furthermore, with 23 touchdown receptions, Moss surpassed Jerry Rice's record, which had stood for 20 years in the NFL. Sadly, the Patriots' fairytale season came to a halt in the Super Bowl when they were defeated by the New York Giants. With 141 touchdown receptions in 2009, Moss surpassed Rice as the NFL's all-time leader.

Being in the penultimate year of his contract and having openly expressed his belief that he was playing in his last year with the Patriots, Moss was moved to the Vikings four games into the 2010 season. His second stay with the Twins was brief—just four games—and was defined by average performance on the field and public criticism of his effort. Following his release from the Vikings' roster, the Tennessee Titans acquired him. Moss announced his retirement from professional football just before the 2011 season began, but he made a triumphant comeback to the league in 2012 after signing with the 49ers of San Francisco. He returned to the Super Bowl in 2013 for the second time in his career, but this time, the 49ers lost to the Ravens of Baltimore. After the Super Bowl, Moss stated his intention to play for another season. After seeing little interest from NFL clubs, he found work as a football commentator on television. The 2018 Pro Football Hall of Fame class included Moss.

92

DEION SANDERS (FOOTBALL)

Deion Sanders is the only athlete to have competed in the Super Bowl and the World Series; he was born on August 9, 1967, in Fort Myers, Florida, USA. Sanders has also coached football and played baseball. Although Sanders was just average as a baseball player, he is generally regarded as the greatest man-to-man cover cornerback in NFL history due to his flamboyant demeanour and outspokenness.

Sanders was a standout athlete in high school, participating on the football, baseball, and track teams, and then attended Florida State University on a full athletic scholarship. As a two-time football All-American, he first gained widespread recognition for his brazen personality. Sanders became a favorite of the sports media in no time at all, but his ostentatious jewelry, tuxedo, and self-promotion—like his 1988 arrival in a white stretch limousine—often overshadowed his great on-field accomplishments. Despite his brash demeanour, the

Atlanta Falcons picked Sanders as the fifth overall pick in the 1989 NFL draft.

Sanders spent most of 1989 in the minor leagues with the New York Yankees, although he did get a 14-game main-level call-up that summer. He was let go by the Yankees in 1990 after hitting 158 in 57 games, and the Atlanta Braves signed him. In 1992, the fast outfielder enjoyed his finest baseball season to date, contributing to the Braves' run to the World Series (a six-game defeat to the Toronto Blue Jays). He led the league with fourteen triples and batted.304. He was moved twice in the 1994 and 1995 seasons, first to the Cincinnati Reds and then to the San Francisco Giants. Sanders sat out 1996, then played with the Reds for a year each in 1997 and 2001 before calling it quits.

Sanders had an enormous influence on his much more fruitful career as a professional football player. He started the season as a full-time starter, earned his first of eight Pro Bowl appearances in his third year, and intercepted five passes in his rookie year. After signing a one-year deal with the 49ers for the 1994 season, he was voted NFL Defensive Player of the Year after contributing to the team's resounding triumph in Super Bowl XXIX and making six interceptions, three of which he returned for touchdowns. He joined the Dallas Cowboys in 1995–96 and won his second Super Bowl that same year. He stayed with the Cowboys for four more seasons until joining the Redskins in 2000. Following a three-year hiatus, Sanders made a triumphant comeback to the NFL in 2006 for a brief appearance with the Baltimore Ravens.

The reason his interception total was lower than that of other top cornerbacks is that defenders would frequently try to avoid throwing the ball to him. However, some have argued that Sanders was not a full-fledged cornerback because of his inconsistent tackling and run-stopping. Sanders had 60 catches throughout his career, three of which were for touchdowns, and his speed and elusiveness made him a top punt and kick returner of all time. He was also a solid offensive option on occasion. At the time of his retirement, he had set an NFL record with 19 non-offensive touchdowns, which included kickoff, punt, interception, and fumble return scores. (In 2014, kick returner Devin Hester shattered his record.)

93

NAOMI OSAKA (TENNIS)

The first Japanese player to win a Grand Slam singles championship was Naomi Osaka, a Japanese tennis player and activist. She thus accomplished her goal after winning the 2018 U.S. Open. Osaka was born on October 16, 1997, in Ōsaka, Japan. Additionally, in 2019, she achieved a first for the Women's Tennis Association (WTA) by being the highest-ranked Asian player. Osaka is also well-known for its commitment to social justice.

The father of Osaka is Haitian, and the mother is Japanese. Her family moved to Long Island, New York, when she was three years old, from Japan, where she was reared. It was there that her dad suggested she try tennis. Osaka was homeschooled at night and played tennis during the day when her family relocated to Florida in 2006. She went straight from junior competition to becoming a professional in 2013, and the Japanese Tennis Association was quick to back her. She then went on to become one of the most exciting young players in the sport in the years that followed. At three separate Grand Slam events in 2016, she reached the round of 32: the Australian Open, the French Open, and the U.S. Open. She set a new record for the fastest serve ever recorded in women's tennis in the last event of that series, reaching 125 mph (201 km/h). In 2016, Osaka was honored by the WTA as the Newcomer of the Year.

Osaka won the BNP Paribas Open at Indian Wells, California, in March of 2018—her first victory on the WTA Tour. About six months later, in the U.S. Open final, she played her childhood hero Serena Williams and won the match in straight sets. In the 2019 Australian Open finals, Osaka defeated Czech Republic's Petra Kvitova in three sets, extending her winning streak to two tournaments. After Williams achieved the feat in 2015, Osaka became the first woman to win consecutive Grand Slam singles championships with her victory. Osaka officially took up the top spot in the world ranking on January 28, 2019. She was number one for twenty-one weeks until Ashleigh Barty of Australia passed her in June. Towards the end of the year, in mid-August, Osaka once again dominated the global standings.

Additionally, Osaka gained a lot of attention for her vocal stances on social justice issues. She took a short break from the 2020 Western & Southern Open tennis event in New York in August to demonstrate her support for the Black Lives Matter demonstrations happening in towns throughout the country at the time. During the COVID-19 outbreak, she donned a set of face masks at the U.S. Open the following month. The masks included the names of African Americans who had died in police shootings or in claimed racially motivated assaults. She said she was trying "to make people start talking" by having them wear masks covering their faces. This was Osaka's second U.S. Open championship, and she won it again. The Associated Press named Osaka 2020 Female Athlete of the Year for her advocacy and tennis prowess.

94

ASHLEIGH BARTY (TENNIS)

For 114 weeks in a row, Ashleigh Barty was ranked number one in women's tennis, and she won 15 singles championships in her career, three of which were at Grand Slam events. Barty was born on April 24, 1996, in Ipswich, Queensland, Australia.

Ipswich, Queensland, Australia, was the place of Barty's birth. His father was an aboriginal Ngaragu man, while his mother was the daughter of English immigrants. At the tender age of five, she picked up tennis and soon became an expert player. She became a member of the ITF junior circuit in her early adolescence. In 2011, she became the youngest Wimbledon champion. After advancing to the WTA Tour two years later, she reached the doubles finals of three Grand Slam tournaments. The Australian Open, Wimbledon, and the U.S. Open were all tournaments in which she and her partner Casey Dellacqua finished in second place. That year, Barty competed in the French Open and the U.S. Open in the singles tournament, where she advanced to the second round. Her versatility and deft touch on the court prompted some to draw parallels between her and Martina Hingis, another tennis prodigy from Switzerland.

But in 2014, Barty shocked everyone by announcing her extended hiatus from tennis after the U.S. Open. Reasons for her hiatus from the public eye included the "general stresses of playing around the world" and the demands of fame. Barty was asked to practice with the Australian women's cricket squad while she was away from tennis. She made the decision to pursue cricket since she showed potential, even though she had never played on a competitive level. She joined the Women's Big Bash League's newest professional squad, the Brisbane Heat, in October 2015. While she was a member of the squad for the 2015–16 season, she eventually made a triumphant comeback to the WTA Tour.

In little time at all, Barty was back to her old tennis self. Her first WTA singles championship came in 2017 when she triumphed at the Malaysian Open. Towards the end of that season, she held the 17th spot globally. Barty advanced to the U.S. Open quarterfinals in the singles tournament in 2018. She and her partner, CoCo Vandeweghe, went on to win the doubles championship later in the event.

Barty was the eighth seed at the 2019 French Open when she arrived in May. After a thrilling three-set semifinal encounter against American Amanda Anisimova, she made it to the finals. Barty became the first Australian woman to win the French Open since Margaret Court in 1973 when she defeated Markéta Vondroušová of the Czech Republic in straight sets in the title match. Two weeks later, Barty won again in the Birmingham Classic in England, solidifying her place atop the WTA world rankings. The 2019 WTA Player of the Year was announced in December by Barty.

In 2020, Barty opted not to defend her title at the French Open. She made the point that performing during the COVID-19 epidemic was dangerous for her health and that the virus had disrupted her training. Though she didn't win a single event that year, she nevertheless managed to finish the season ranked first in the world. Barty advanced to the Wimbledon finals in July 2021 and won in three sets against Czech Republic's Karolína Plíšková. Barty became the first Australian woman to win the Wimbledon singles championship since Evonne Goolagong Cawley in 1980 with her triumph.

95

SIDNEY CROSBY (HOCKEY)

Canadian ice hockey player Sidney Crosby became the youngest captain of an NHL club in 2007 and captained the Pittsburgh Penguins to three Stanley Cup victories (in 2009, 2016, and 2017). Crosby was born on August 7, 1987, in Cole Harbour, Nova Scotia, Canada.

The Montreal Canadiens selected Crosby, whose father was a goalie, and Crosby learned to skate at the age of three. While a sophomore in high school in Faribault, Minnesota, he played in 57 games and had 72 goals and 90 assists. Wayne Gretzky, a giant in the ice hockey world, took notice of Crosby's achievement and thought that he would eventually break his own records. In 121 regular-season games over two years, Crosby scored 120 goals and tallied 183 assists after being recruited by the Quebec Major Junior Hockey League side Rimouski Océanic in 2003. He was rated Canada's best junior player year after year. In addition, he became the youngest player in Canadian national junior hockey history to score a goal after joining the squad.

At the age of eighteen, Crosby was the first overall choice in the 2005 NHL draft by the Pittsburgh Penguins. With so many people comparing Crosby to Gretzky, the young player's expectations were high. Crosby was even given the moniker "The Next One," a play on Gretzky's "The Great One" moniker. Crosby became the youngest player in NHL history to accomplish the feat at the conclusion of his rookie season (2005–06) when he scored 100 points (goals plus assists).

Crosby set even more records in his second season. The Art Ross Trophy was bestowed to him as the youngest winner ever for his 120 points scored in 79 games. He became the second-youngest player in NHL history to win the Hart Trophy as the league's most valuable player, and he became the youngest player to have a six-point game since Gretzky in 1980. When Crosby became the Penguins' captain in 2007, he became the NHL's youngest captain ever. With Crosby's aid, the Penguins reached the Stanley Cup finals in 2007–08. Unfortunately, they were defeated in six games by the Detroit Red Wings. The next season, Crosby had 103 points, enough for third place in the NHL. The Penguins met the Red Wings in the playoffs again, but this time they won in seven games.

After suffering a concussion in January 2011 after an on-ice collision, his career almost ended too soon. There was concern that Crosby's post-concussion issues might keep him out of hockey for the rest of the 2010–11 season. In November 2011, Crosby returned to the Penguins' lineup after a lengthy recuperation. However, he only played for two weeks before experiencing a recurrence of symptoms similar to a concussion, once again sidelining him. He came back in March of 2012. The public's focus on player safety in the NHL shifted after his injuries received a lot of media attention.

Despite sitting out 12 games due to a fractured jaw during the 2012–13 NHL season due to the lockout, Crosby still averaged 1.56 points per game, good for first in the league. Even though Crosby went scoreless in that series, the Boston Bruins swept the top-seeded Penguins in the subsequent playoffs. In addition to his second Hart Trophy, he won the Art Ross Trophy for leading the NHL in points with 104 in the 2013–14 season. Still, he struggled to find the back of the net in the playoffs, with just one goal and eight assists in thirteen playoff games as the Penguins lost in the conference semifinals. Even though Crosby had his worst point total of the season (84) in 2014–15 (a season unaffected by injury or labor troubles), he still led the NHL in points per game (1.09). Despite having a lot of skill on the roster, the Penguins suffered another poor season, this time losing in the first round of the playoffs despite barely making it.

96

TERENCE CRAWFORD (BOXING)

Debbie and Terry Crawford had Terence Allen Crawford on September 28, 1987, in Omaha, Nebraska. At Bryan High School, he grew interested in boxing, which became his profession. Crawford realized his gift in junior high. His trainer often organized battles to calm agitated teens at key periods.

"Bud liked to see you hurt," says his trainer. Young Bud became empowered as a preteen and adolescent.

Bud is gentle but a nasty beast in the ring. He enjoys another's agony, which is rare for a combatant. Disrespectful actions or comments from another opponent lead to further rounds and more injuries and humiliations. Bud had a good boxing career. ESPN twice named him boxer of the year and the BWA once.

Crawford is the world's second-most active boxer since 2018. He defended the first man boxer to simultaneously hold the WBA, WBC, IBF, and WBO world championships.

Terence Crawford defeated Brian Cummings in the first round of his 2008 professional debut. His battles weren't memorable until he met former WBO lightweight Champion Breidis Prescott between Brandon Rios and Mike Alvarado.

Crawford said he won $125,000 by hitting Prescott into a cocked hat. In 2013, The American defeated Alejandro Sanabria in Texas to win the WBO and NABO lightweight belts. Crawford faced WBO titleholder Andrey Klimov in a ten-round elimination battle.

Crawford defeated the Russian in 10 rounds by unanimous decision, handing him his first professional loss.

Crawford was defending his championship against Yuriokis Gamboa in his maiden professional bout in Omaha, Nebraska.

The former unified featherweight champion and 2004 Cuban Olympic gold winner was the favorite to enter the match. Although fast, Gamboa dominated the early rounds. Crawford adjusted and defeated Gamboa in the fifth, eighth, and two ninth rounds via TKO.

In 2014, Terence Crawford claimed Yuriokis Gamboa's bout was his toughest. Crawford would defend his WBO championship against Ray Beltran in Omaha, Nebraska, his hometown, in November 2014.

The winner becomes The Ring's lightweight champion. The judges declared the American the victor following another unanimous, kind judgement.

Bud announced his move from lightweight to light welterweight after the match. ESPN and the Boxing Writers Association of America named Terence Crawford 2014's Fighter of the Year.

97

NAOYA INOUE (BOXING)

Four-division world champion Inoue has won championships at light flyweight, flyweight, super flyweight, and bantamweight. His WBC and WBO championships make him the super bantamweight world champion.

Naoya Inoue is one of the most feared boxers, with a 92% knockout rate. This boxer is smart and knows the sport well.

Inoue is a world-class boxer and popular in Japan. His example inspires young people and sportsmen worldwide.

Additional biographical information on Naoya Inoue:

Naoya Inoue was born into boxing. His brother, Takuma Inoue, and father, Shingo Inoue, were professional boxers.

He began boxing at four and has trained ever since. He became professional in 2012 and progressed fast. He is the current unified super bantamweight world champion after winning world championships in three prior weight classes.

He is a world-class boxer noted for his aggressive approach and powerful knockout power. Japan considers him a national hero and popular character. Inoue is a champion and one of the most interesting fighters today.

Naoya Inoue's father, Shingo, was a boxer. The family link was Naoya's first move towards boxing immortality.

Inoue followed his father into sports at age 5. He was gifted from the start and improved as he learned the sweet science.

The 2012 boxing debut of Inoue was his first major accomplishment. He immediately became famous and won several games. The moniker "The Monster" made sense when the boxing world noticed this growing Japanese star.

He won the WBC Light Flyweight championship in his sixth professional bout after rising quickly. In these early fights, Inoue showed his accuracy, quickness, and hitting force. Opponents and fans were astonished by his quick, decisive wins.

In 2018, Inoue entered the World Boxing Super Series (WBSS) Bantamweight event, his international breakthrough. In this famous tournament, he fought the greatest competitors in his weight class and showed his skills.

He defeated former WBA champion Juan Carlos Payano in the quarterfinals with a stunning first-round knockout. Inoue then knocked off Emmanuel Rodriguez in the second round to set up a thrilling final against Nonito Donaire.

The final versus Donaire tested Inoue's toughness. The bout ran twelve rounds as Donaire, a world champion, pushed Inoue to his utmost. Inoue won the World Boxing Super Series and became a world champion.

Inoue rose to worldwide boxing prominence after winning the WBSS final. His battle performance and perseverance caught the attention of boxing commentators and fans worldwide.

Inoue was successful not just because of his technical talents and knockout power but also because of his work ethic and commitment. He was a worldwide boxing celebrity, not simply a Japanese one.

After winning the WBSS, Inoue maintained his bantamweight domination. IBF and Ring Magazine titles were added to his collection. His boxing achievements showed his dedication to perfection and ambition to change the sport.

The latest update shows Naoya Inoue unbeaten in his professional career, with many world championships and a high knockout rate. He still wants to be great in a sport where legends are produced.

Inoue's path is about winning hearts as well as trophies. He is a Japanese sports hero and a global boxing role model. His work ethic, sportsmanship, and enthusiasm in every battle have won many admirers.

98

TYSON FURY (BOXING)

Tyson Fury made his pro debut in December 2008 with a first-round TKO victory against Hungarian Bela Gyongyosi. He won six more knockouts in 2009. The world was drawn to Fury's unconventional style, technique, range, and character, and he won the English, British, and Commonwealth titles before vacating to win the Irish title and climbing the ranks to reach the world title.

Tyson's life changed in 2015 in ways the boxing world didn't predict. Team Fury knew Tyson could defeat 11-year undefeated Wladimir Klitschko and win the world's undisputed heavyweight title in Dusseldorf in November. After a buildup of trash-talk and mind games and a near delay due to a canvas dispute on fight weekend, the world witnessed the rangy, unpredictable underdog outboxing the champion for 12 rounds before winning unanimously on distant soil.

After winning the WBA, IBF, WBO, IBO, Lineal, and The Ring Heavyweight belts and reaching the top of his profession, Tyson fell into well-publicized melancholy.

Fury realized things needed to change in 2017, bringing light into the darkness. Tyson decided enough was enough at 28 stone and started his recovery alongside his loving wife, Paris, his family, and God.

His amazing narrative and mental health transparency touched people worldwide. The refreshing mental health activism from a renowned combat sportsman gave more people hope and connection in their challenges. Conversations began in unexpected places, and Tyson Fury became a global mental health advocate.

Tyson trained for more than fitness and depression. After two warm-up bouts, he faced WBC World Heavyweight Champion Deontay Wilder, The Bronze Bomber, and his lethal right hand.

That shocked the globe and became one of the greatest talking points in modern boxing history. It ended in a draw, with many fans feeling Tyson did enough to win and bring the title back to the UK. Wilder's iconic power shot on Fury's chin, seeing the Gipsy King fall to the canvas, seemingly out cold, only for Fury to rise to his feet to beat the 10-count, may have saved him with a draw. The world saw Fury's desire to beat the count as a sign that anybody might overcome sadness.

Public opinion changed. Fury reclaimed his title after defeating Wilder in two more bouts, completing one of the finest trilogies in history. Fury has also become a worldwide brand and businessman, speaking up for mental health and reclaiming his life as a husband and father to his six children in Morecambe, England.

99

STEPHEN CURRY (BASKETBALL)

Stephen Curry is an American professional basketball player. He joined the Golden State Warriors in 2014–15, 2016–17, 2017–18, and 2021–22. In 2015–16, Curry helped the Warriors achieve the best regular-season record in NBA history with 73 wins.

Because his father, sharpshooter Dell Curry, was an NBA veteran for 16 years, Curry had a basketball-centric upbringing. From his father, the younger Curry inherited the game's complexities. College scouts were not swayed by his impressive shooting and good "basketball IQ" despite his stocky build and mediocre 6-foot (1.8-meter) height. Davidson (North Carolina) institution, which had an enrollment of less than 2,000 students, was his institution of choice despite the lack of scholarship offers from big collegiate basketball programmes. He had an immediate impact, however, leading all first-year players in the nation with 21.5 points per game. As a sophomore, Curry shot to fame with an unbelievable performance that included what would become his trademark shot—a three-pointer from far out—and led 10th-seeded Davidson to the Elite Eight of the National Collegiate Athletic Association men's top-division basketball championship tournament. The shot went viral. Despite the lack of heroics in the playoffs during his junior year, he still managed to lead the nation in scoring average at 28.6 points per game and was selected as a unanimous first-team All-American. After that, he went into the 2009 NBA draft, where the Warriors took him seventh overall.

In his first year with the Warriors, Curry became the starting point guard and averaged 17.5 points per game, making an instant impression. Curry had ligament surgery in the offseason after suffering a string of ankle injuries that limited him to 26 games during the 2011–12 season. The Warriors were able to assemble a strong roster around their rising star after he inked a modest four-year $44 million agreement. In 2012–13, Curry made 272 three-pointers, more than any other player in the NBA. He was named to his first All-Star team the following season after accomplishing the same thing (with 261). While guiding the Warriors to a then-best 67-15 record in the NBA in 2014–15, he set a new record with 286 three-pointers and was awarded the league's MVP. In the next playoffs, Curry led the Warriors to their first championship in four decades, defeating the Cleveland Cavaliers.

With Curry at the helm, the Warriors reached new heights in 2015–16, as they finished the regular season with 76 wins, one more than the 1995–96 Chicago Bulls. Not only did he make an unprecedented 402 three-pointers, but he also averaged 30.1 points per game, which was great for the NBA. Curry became the first player to ever be selected MVP by a unanimous vote, and he won the award for the second year in a row. An unexpected letdown came at the conclusion of the Warriors' spectacular season when they let the Cavaliers take a 3-1 lead in the NBA playoffs.

The 2016–17 season was Curry's fifth consecutive season as the NBA leader in three-point field goals made (324) and the Warriors' second consecutive season as the league's best-winning team (67). After a record-setting 12-game winning streak to start the playoffs, Golden State won the Western Conference for the third year in a row. After suffering their first playoff setback in NBA Finals Game 4, the Warriors rallied to beat the Cavaliers in five games and win Curry's second NBA championship.

100

KEVIN DURANT (BASKETBALL)

American professional basketball player Kevin Durant was born on September 29, 1988, in Washington, D.C., USA. He earned the 2013–14 NBA MVP award and became one of the greatest players of his generation while still in his early twenties.

In his early years of high school, Durant had already established himself as one of the top prospects in the flourishing Washington, D.C.-area basketball scene, and by his senior year, he had become an All-American. He played college basketball at U.T., where he set freshman scoring (25.6 ppg), rebounding (11.1 ppg), and blocked shot (67) records for the Big 12 Conference. He made history as the first freshman to win consensus national college player of the year awards and was also named to the All-American first team. After deciding to forego his last year of college, he entered the 2007 NBA draft with the second overall selection by the Seattle SuperSonics.

The city of Seattle declined to support the team's new owners' desire for a publicly subsidized arena, and the prospect of the team's relocation turned off many fans. However, Durant stood out as an exception during his rookie year. With a scoring average of 20.3 per game, Durant easily won the NBA Rookie of the Year title that season. Despite his electrifying performance, the Sonics' relationship with the community remained strained, and they relocated to the Oklahoma community, becoming the Thunder at the conclusion of the season. In his second season with the new team, Durant showed no ill effects from the move, improving his statistics in scoring, rebounds, assists and steals. While leading the Thunder to their first-ever postseason participation in their new arena in 2009–10, he started a run of five consecutive All-Star Game appearances and was named to the NBA first team. With Durant averaging 28.5 points per game in the playoffs in 2011–12, the Thunder made it to the NBA finals. Unfortunately, they were defeated in a five-game series by the Miami Heat.

As Durant worked on his outside game, the 6-foot-9-inch (2.06-meter) forward became a more formidable opponent. Durant could tower over lesser guards and shoot over or run past lumbering post players. Durant, who began his dominant play in the 2009–10 season, went on to lead the NBA in scoring average four times and total points five times (finishing second in 2012–13). In the 2013–14 season, when he was named the league's most valuable player, he averaged a career-high 32 points, 5.5 assists, and 7.4 rebounds per game. Durant had a right foot injury the previous season and had a rocky road to return, limiting him to only 27 games. In 2015–16, he got back on track with a career-high 8.2 rebounds per game to go along with his 28.2 points per game. After a 3-1 series lead, Oklahoma City was defeated in seven games by the Golden State Warriors in the conference finals, despite Durant's best efforts. The Warriors had established an NBA record with 73 wins in the regular season. Durant surprised the NBA the next offseason when he signed with the Warriors instead of the Thunder during free agency.

Playing with the Warriors in 2016–17—the most talented squad he has ever been a part of—Durant maintained his stellar performance, averaging 25.1 points per game and contributing to Golden State's 67 victories. The Warriors then won the Western Conference and broke an NBA record with 12 consecutive wins to start the playoffs. In the NBA Finals, the Warriors' dominance continued as they dropped just one game against the Cleveland Cavaliers and won the league title. As a result of his outstanding play in the finals, Durant was awarded Most Valuable Player. He averaged 35.2 points per game.

*****